Women in Southern Culture

Margaret Ripley Wolfe, SERIES EDITOR

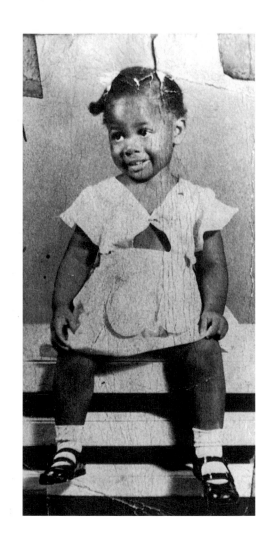

Multicolored Memories of a Black Southern Girl

KITTY OLIVER

THE UNIVERSITY PRESS OF KENTUCKY

Publication of this volume was made possible in part
by a grant from the National Endowment for the Humanities.

Published by The University Press of Kentucky.
Scholarly publisher for the Commonwealth,
serving Bellarmine University, Berea College, Centre
College of Kentucky, Eastern Kentucky University,
The Filson Historical Society, Georgetown College,
Kentucky Historical Society, Kentucky State University,
Morehead State University, Murray State University,
Northern Kentucky University, Transylvania University,
University of Kentucky, University of Louisville,
and Western Kentucky University.

Editorial and Sales Offices: The University Press of Kentucky
663 South Limestone Street, Lexington, Kentucky 40508–4008

05   04   03   02   01   5   4   3   2   1

Frontispiece: Kitty Oliver at two years of age.

Library of Congress Cataloging-in-Publication Data
Oliver, Kitty, 1947-
    Multicolored memories of a Black Southern girl / Kitty Oliver.
        p. cm. — (Women in Southern culture)
     ISBN 0-8131-2208-2 (cloth : alk. paper)
     1. Oliver, Kitty, 1947- —Childhood and youth. 2. African American women—
Florida—Jacksonville—Biography. 3. African Americans—Florida—Jacksonville—
Biography. 4. Jacksonville (Fla.)—Biography. 5. Oliver, Kitty, 1947- —Family.
6. African American women journalists—Biography. 7. Jacksonville (Fla.)—Race
relations. 8. African Americans—Florida—Social conditions—20th century.
9. African Americans—Florida--Social life and customs—20th century.
10. Pluralism (Social sciences)—Florida. I. Title. II. Series.
     F319.J1 O45 2001
     975.9'12063'092—dc21

CONTENTS

EDITOR'S PREFACE

Women in Southern Culture is dedicated to the experience of women across the vast range of southern history, those consigned to the margins of history as well as those in the mainstream. The publication of Kitty Oliver's *Multicolored Memories of a Black Southern Girl* follows Linda Scott DeRosier's *Creeker: A Woman's Journey* and moves the series from the hollows of eastern Kentucky to the streets of Jacksonville, Florida. Incorporating memories from the author's childhood and youth of the 1950s and 1960s, this autobiography draws on a diverse family heritage that is deeply rooted in the rural South. Nevertheless, the author herself has known an urban existence. Once with the *Miami Herald* and now at Florida Atlantic University, Kitty Oliver may well be the most powerful black female writer to emerge from the Sunshine State since Zora Neale Hurston.

Comedy and tragedy, the ordinary and extraordinary, await the reader in *Multicolored Memories of a Black Southern Girl*. The pages reveal an often lonely soul sustained by food, music, curiosity, and love. Within her family hierarchy, a "Geechee" grandfather is a significant but somewhat mysterious presence, a shadowy father lurks about, and an indomitable mother earns top billing. Raising a daughter mostly alone, she takes pride in being a black woman who has "papers" on her man. Confronted with the uncertainties of her only child leaving home to enroll at the newly integrated University of Florida, she rises above her personal fears. "I've been thinking about it," she confides. "If my folks had let me go to a nursing school out of town like I wanted, my life would have turned out so much better." The voice "from far away" had given its permission.

Oliver's narrative evokes the sights, sounds, and smells of a vibrant black culture on the brink of disintegration when racial barriers crumbled. As one of the first black freshmen to attend the University of Florida, the author faced and met challenges of desegregation, crossing boundaries that involved class as well as color. Furthermore, from the inside out, Oliver has clearly delineated internal divisions and social distinctions within the black community that are often more obscure than obvious to the white world. Told without rancor, this story speaks directly to the black female experience of Kitty Oliver's generation. It is moving because of what it reveals about the pathos of an individual life in a certain time and place; it is memorable because some strands of this uniquely personal journey are so common to the shared human drama.

Margaret Ripley Wolfe

ACKNOWLEDGMENTS

The idea for this book started in workshops at Florida International University's Creative Writing Program, headed by Les Standiford, circa 1994. I want to thank Lynne Barrett, Meri-Jane Rochelson, John Dufresne, and John Ernest for seeing something in my work and encouraging further exploration; Dan Wakefield, Mark Gauert, and Mary Jane Ryals for urging me on; Lisa Lupari and Candace West for their photos; and Margaret Ripley Wolfe for the kindest editing touch on these words.

Thanks to my rainbow of sister-friends just for being in my life—Lynn Laurenti, Carole Taylor, Lyn Kurpiewski, Kathryn Mickle, and Janie DeVos, especially, for the loving reader's eye.

May my children, Kali and Brian, and my grandson Jordan remember as well and enjoy carrying the memories on and on. And most of all, my love and gratitude to Mama, Terotha Elizabeth Glover Leeks, for the legacy of stories that started it all.

Chapter 1, titled "Migrations," first appeared in *Kestrel* magazine; portions of some chapters originally appeared as articles in the *Sun-Sentinel*, Fort Lauderdale, Florida.

PART ONE

Those Sapphire, Ruby and Pearl girls come here knowing

Sometimes

You've got to stop

and turn around

to get where you're going.

—Kitty Oliver

MIGRATIONS

*F*or as long as I can remember, I have had a preference for traveling by train because the experience of the journey is more prolonged. Schedules are only estimates; hours expand. There is plenty of time to weigh and mull over one's life. Once the coach lurches forward and the engine accelerates to top speed, a familiar crosscurrent of sensations kicks in. I know I am in transit, headed somewhere, but at the same time I feel suspended. The world is moving—without me. For amusement I play "camera," framing wide shots in the window and sometimes zooming in on one image as the rest of the scenery whizzes past. A flock of egrets blankets a field. An abandoned car is scorched by the heat. An old man sits under a tree and strips the hull off a stalk of sugarcane. The scenes pop up sporadically in the otherwise monotonous interior of Florida along the south-north stretch of passenger railroad tracks. I have taken the eight-hour ride from Fort Lauderdale, where I live, back to Jacksonville, where I was born, numerous times to visit my mother. But the destination this time is farther north. After a business stop in Charleston, South Carolina, I am headed west seventy miles to visit a little town called Allendale, where my mother's parents were born and raised. As night shades the windows and iron wheels click off the miles, I cannot help but ponder how far away I have traveled all these years just to arrive back at this point.

Every family has its maverick—the one who runs counter to the herd—and I played that role in mine. I was the first grandkid and an only child. Among my cousins, I was much older and estranged from the others, and I was the one who left home and stayed away. In 1965, I climbed on a Greyhound bus and took off for the newly integrated University of Florida, aware that a new chapter of racial history was being written for people of my generation. Some of us blacks were making the first tentative steps into mainstream America, and we met up with some whites who were trying to make room for us. I went from listening to The Drifters and James Brown to Jefferson Airplane and Jimi Hendrix; from being "colored" and "Negro" to being "black." So many new things were happening, what did the past matter? But the past kept dogging me in odd, surprising ways.

That first evening on campus, I stood in the dormitory dining hall during a reception for freshmen and their parents. As I hovered near the punch bowl, refilling my glass and chewing crackers I did not taste, enigmatic couples—older arms draped protectively around the shoulders of sons and daughters—glided past. In foreign territory, I felt doused with the scent of fear. A white girl with a bouncy brown pageboy and a name tag that read "Resident Assistant" chatted her way around the room and over to me. We shared names and college majors—mine was English; *I learned to read and write,* I would quip many years later. After a few awkward moments, the upperclassman asked where I was from and I said that I was from Jacksonville. She was from Lake City, not too far from me, she said, becoming animated again. Her family had lived there for three or four generations, nearly owned the town. She was the third person in her family to attend the University of Florida. And what about me? Where were my people from? My answer came out uneasily, perhaps a bit curt. "From *Jacksonville,*" I repeated. But that was too brief a history. The truth was that I knew very little about my family heritage beyond the painful reality that my great-grandparents had been legally called chattel. I thought of adding "and Africa," although that seemed even more vague. But the brown-haired girl had given up on conversation and walked away.

At some point I decided just to consider myself a product of the civil rights movement, of integration and the promises it held. *I am a future person,* I started saying. This new self-image sharpened my critical edge. Sometimes my white friends forgot themselves in my company and slipped into nostalgic musings about the graciousness of the Old South. I reminded them of the brutality of slave owners, which had warped those reputed antebellum charms. When black friends or acquaintances lapsed into longing for the economic independence and community solidity of the pre-integration days, I countered with a longer list of inequities that blacks had suffered in segregation during that time. I was quick to point out that only certain people had fared well. Later, as a journalist, I would interview many immigrants to this country and observe how the poignancy of memory clogged their throats and stung their eyes. A snatch of the old language, some custom, some ritual bound them to their heritage and to the past. I admired their sinewy ties to home and envied their emotional connection, even if they had to gloss over the problems they fled, yet I could not relate to their feelings.

But life has a way of subtly reshaping one's perspective. When I married, I gained scores of in-laws. On holidays and in the summer, we either spent time with some of my husband's family or on the phone explaining why we could not. We had two children, and as they grew they asked harder, more penetrating questions. One year, after attending a reunion of the extended family, my son cornered me in the kitchen with questions. He must have been close to ten years old at the time. He wanted to understand the web of interrelationships of one set of people he had met at the gathering. "Actually, those kids aren't really your cousins," I explained. "They're your uncle's first wife's children by her second husband. And she's not your aunt, but she used to be." It was getting complicated, even to me. He sighed, fed up. "I'll just call them all relatives." Then he cocked his head with a look of concern. "What about *your* people, Mom?" The question triggered the latch of some rusty chamber of my brain that I had sealed off a long time ago. Although I was caught off guard, information spouted out—sparse but automatic, "Well, Grandma Tee and I were born in Jacksonville, but my grandparents were Geechees from South Carolina." Then the spigot ran dry. "What's a Geechee?" he asked. My eyes avoided his, but I stammered on. "Oh . . . they talk funny, and they love to eat rice." That is all I could come up with. His daylight of a smile broke open. "*I* love to eat rice," he chimed in. Satisfied with that discovery, he grabbed a banana, jumped on his bike, and pedaled off to play with his friends. I was left to sort out the rush of childhood memories suddenly stirred up by the word I had just introduced him to.

I first heard the word "Geechee" one night at my grandparents' house after dinner, when they got into one of those arguments I knew would lead to an early bedtime for me. I do not know how old I was then, but I remember how my grandfather stewed in the living room with his chin-in-the-hand, "leave-me-alone" look and stared at the test pattern on the television waiting for the six o'clock evening news to come on. I stayed at the kitchen table while my step-grandmother brimmed over with anger as she doled out my dessert. Usually she counted two spoonfuls of sliced peaches, no more. But this time she kept dipping into the can, muttering in a voice just low enough to stay within the kitchen walls. As the juice overflowed I sat ready to pounce and lick the sides of the bowl when I felt the tart-tongued sting. "You old *Geechee,* you!" She hurled it toward the living room with a string of epithets, but this one bounced right back on me. I knew it was an insult, but something about the strange new word reverberated with intrigue. Later at home I prodded Mama for more information, but her response was clouded by an odd tension as discomfort crept into her voice. "I went there a couple of summers when I was a little girl, but I don't remember anything about it except that it was in the country." Her eyes narrowed. "I was born in Jacksonville. I don't know anything about that place." Discussion closed.

But the taste of that sweet-and-sour word had obviously lingered, long after integration lured me away and I had begun raising children of my own. As more years passed, I also became aware of other familial forces at work. My mother, once the rebellious baby of the family, was quickly ascending to the role of family elder as my grandparents' generation passed on. And like it or not, I was in training, next in line. Age was catching up with my generation. We were enrolling kids in college, or sometimes nursery school, at the same time we were sending parents to nursing homes or planning their funerals. The past was becoming more important because we had lived long enough to have one of our own. Some of my friends were starting to plan their vacations around family reunions—even to organize them. Others marveled that they had much more patience and respect for elderly relatives than they did when they were younger. They spent time visiting, probing for information, poking at the branches of the family tree with interest. It was our turn to keep the stories alive for posterity. For one of the first generation of blacks who emigrated into the white world and assimilated, however, this search has taken on a troubling significance. I am a displaced person without a motherland. But I have made a career as a writer chronicling other people's lives and cultures, and now I want to learn something about that part of my past that has been a mystery to me most of my life. Hence this journey. I expect to unearth roots or to bury them for good. The train I ride on jerks and pulls sluggishly away from another station, and ever so steadily it picks up speed.

The Jacksonville, Florida, I grew up in had its pretty face on the beaches along the Atlantic Ocean, but it was really just a homely working-class town. People made paper and boxes, ground grits and coffee, shipped fruit, packed meat, and cleaned shrimp. They bought and sold at the farmer's market. Blacks were confined to three areas separated by highways and bridges, each with its own churches, schools, and attitude. For those who lived in my urban area, the south-side folks were dismissed as faraway rural people who lived in trailers and frame houses and needed a car to get anywhere. We saw them once a year at football games when they arrived to beat our team and then disappear into the woods again. The east-siders were scrappy rivals but small-town suburbanites by comparison, with their aging buildings and five-and-dime corner stores in the gaping shadow of football in what was then called the Gator Bowl. But we lived just one short bus ride to downtown, and all the Saturday night action happened on our side. The city maps say north side, but we called ourselves west-siders to distinguish ourselves from those "others" across town.

Often when people recall the era of segregation as a time when communities were unified, nurturing, and egalitarian, I wonder where they lived. I must have come of age during the waning days. There might have been an absence of racial contrast, but there was certainly no absence of conflict. This was a time when richly diverse, opposing energies fermented and we reveled in the fact that there were all kinds of black people constantly jockeying for a superior position. In this self-centered community, we listened to the black radio station WOBS for music and information and daydreamed over stories in *Bronze Star* romance magazine. The local white newspaper ran two "Colored Pages" once a week, in a back section, where we read about births, deaths, and marriages, but for the juicy news we read the *Florida Star*. The streets vibrated with music, aromas, and bright clothes in bold combinations bought from stores found only in our neighborhoods that catered only to us. Noises spilled out of apartments onto porches and sidewalks, and neighbors had a survival sense of when they'd better just listen and when to complain. Like pockets of Italians, Irish, Jews, or Cubans found in other cities—or any community where people are the same color, religion, or language—we may have looked pretty much homogeneous from the outside. Our confinement, of course, was even more complete because it was enforced by Jim Crow segregation laws. But human nature can be resourceful, even under the worst of conditions. In isolation, we divided ourselves as though we lived in the only real world.

Bisecting the heart of the city was the St. Johns River, one of the few in the world that flows north instead of south, we were taught. My neighborhood was a similar anomaly. Some of the people who were a part of the great migration of blacks from the farms of the Deep South after World War I must have gotten disoriented; in particular, the people from South Carolina, Georgia, and Alabama. Instead of heading north like most southern blacks, they flocked even farther south. Maybe there was just something about the southern life they felt rooted to, or maybe they just did not believe that prospects were better for them in the North. I figured it was the latter, judging by what I saw during the rare times relatives from "up there" visited us when I was a little girl.

Days ahead you could smell when a northerner was coming to town. Pots of greens with ham hocks and neck bones instead of just fatback overflowed on some mother's stove. Hair sizzled from the gobs of grease used to straighten and curl a style that would not look nappy during the relative's visit. Perspiring youngsters and their friends worked like day laborers, huddled around record players and 45s, practicing the Slide, the Mashed Potato, and the Hully Gully to prove to their teenage cousins that they were not really hicks. The guests arrived, usually by train, lugging gifts of clothes and kitchen appliances, and their hosts showed them off to neighbors like curios. I remember sitting on a porch a few doors down from our house with the grown-ups while they talked. The other little girls played hopscotch or shot marbles; I was more interested in listening. Everything was bigger, better, and more sophisticated in "Philly, D.C., Chicago, or New *Yourrrrk*," the visitors bragged while sucking on crab legs and slurping watermelon as though they were starving. They said, "The money is great, child. You can really make it up there." But most of them worked two or three jobs. They talked fast, as if they had to use every word they knew, and they accented syllables that we usually drawled or dropped. But every once in awhile their tongues got all tangled up and started fighting with their words. When they split infinitives and mangled pronunciations, the neighbors caught it like players on the sidelines who had finally got their turn. They winked and elbowed each other. Later they gossiped and hissed "stuck up" and "phony, child" to pump up their egos again.

On the other hand, a steady flow of Deep South southerners was still arriving when I was a kid, and the attitude toward them was quite different. We snickered the message in school hallways, whispered it behind church fans, and taunted it from street corners. The worst thing you could be accused of was looking, acting, or talking "country," which is what the immigrants were called. Their behavior, such as traveling with paper bags instead of luggage, was embarrassing. You could tell they were uneducated because they said "dat dere" and "deez." They wore home-sewn or hand-me-down "mammy-made" clothes. At home, I was reprimanded to "Hold your head up when you talk, girl" and "Stop grinning like a fool." That was behavior unbecoming a city girl.

But behind the closed doors of our families' lives we also had a few odd behaviors of our own, superstitions we observed as part of everyday life but I did not dare share with my city friends. As a baby I wore a penny with a hole drilled in it, dangling around my neck, to make me cut teeth. Sardine grease was rubbed on my neck to relieve the aftereffects of the mumps. Garlic was always in the house, not just as a spice but as a good-luck charm. If your nose itched, company was coming—right nostril for a man, left for a woman; when your ears burned, someone was talking about you. Your right hand itched because you were getting money; your left because you were getting mail. Dreams had to be told the next morning, then interpreted in a dream book to find the corresponding numbers that could win in bolita (a form of numbers pool) that week. The *Farmer's Almanac* was consulted to determine the phases of the moon before any medical help was sought; for example, no dental work when the sign (or phase) of the moon was in the head, or you would either bleed profusely or certainly have a lot of pain. Once I remember straining to decipher the whispered voices of my mother and her friends in our living room, and I heard the story of a root-working that was done on a woman they knew. "Her legs swelled up like a balloon," one of the women said. "That thing burst and maggots crawled out." I heard my mother's ominous voice say, "Child, that's stuff you don't mess with." The image was scarier to me than any horror movie, and I knew it was not a city-bred fear.

Based on the tidbits I was told of our family story, I began to see that our roots were decidedly country. My mother's parents were part of that early wave of settlers from South Carolina. Her mother died at twenty-four after bearing three daughters (one died in infancy), and her father remarried a Florida-born woman. This South Carolina man, my grandfather, left his home at 6:00 A.M. every Tuesday, his day off, to go fishing, taking the joy with him. Rice was always a side dish on the dinner table in accompaniment to the fried or smothered mullet, whiting, or trout he caught. He was a railroad man, who set his pocket watch by the arrival whistles of the Seaboard and Atlantic Coastline runs, and he was always a curiosity to me. "Foot to Foot" he nicknamed me, because whenever I visited his house I followed him around asking questions. As soon as he washed up after work servicing cars in the railway yards, I would climb onto his lap. I loved to rub my hands across his clean-shaven, rubber-ball head and slide my smooth cheek along the stubble on his almost as much as I loved to talk. Sheepishly, like an awkward schoolboy, he returned my hugs and endured my chatter. "How do the train wheels stay on the tracks instead of falling off, Bubba? I bet they have really big shoes," I would ponder. "What would happen if the light went out in the sun? Huh?" When he got bored, he would shove me away gruffly with, "Leave me alone now, I'm tired." And I did, immediately. He was crisp brown as the last leaves of fall, and at barely five feet five he was short—like his temper when he was irritated or crossed. I always say I got my love of trains from him.

As we pass through the Jacksonville station where I usually get off to visit my mother, I lean back in my seat, trying not to think too much about what is ahead. I've been told that my first trip on a train was from Jacksonville to South Carolina when I was in preschool. What I remember is the pounding sound, like horseshoes on a metal road, and falling asleep with the side-to-side rocking motion. I still find the ride as comforting as my mother's arms. A woman I saw on that first visit to South Carolina is one of the earliest and most vivid images from my childhood. She was short, like an elf, with a head scarf knotted above her leathery forehead. As she stood in the screenless doorway of her house, I guess, waving and getting smaller all the time as we rode away, she called out, "*Me disah oneah heah.*" She was probably talking to someone else who I did not see or no longer remember, summoning the person or trying to get his attention, pointing out something like "this one here" nearby. I am not sure. What I do recall, however, is the urgency of the sound. I can now identify it best as a patois akin to the speech of rural people I have heard converse in the mountains of Jamaica—akin to village Africans, not the ones with a British education. The woman, I learned later, was my mother's aunt, her mother's only sister, and she died not long after my visit. The high-pitched rhythm of her Geechee voice that day scratched the air, tickling my ears, and it has forever stayed in my memory.

I recall that voice now on this trip, along with the other information I have dug up about these Geechees over the years, and I am starting to get excited now by the possibilities. I remind myself not to use the term "Geechee" when I talk to people, though. At least not at first, I have been cautioned. They might get offended. The proper name, I have been told, is "Gullah." The word refers to people from the sea islands off the coasts of South Carolina and Georgia. A few of these people are still around, and there is a movement to preserve their culture as it is maintained in isolation on the few islands that have not yet been purchased by resort developers. These people are the direct descendants of slaves who were shipped from the West Coast of Africa to work primarily on rice plantations or to pick cotton and indigo. When slavery ended, they worked for wages in the phosphate industries and as farm laborers. But mostly they stayed to themselves.

That patois I remember seemed like just a jumble of singsong sounds, yet it was understandable, too, perhaps because of the mixture of African dialects and English. The research I have read says the Gullah people hold closely to African folk traditions, but a few of the strange traditions sound pretty American-like and familiar to me. In our neighborhood, though, we just called them "funny" ways. If a man walked down the street with the fly of his trousers open, mumbling to himself, the average person might think he was mentally ill. But some of the people I knew would swear, "Poor thing, somebody's been messing with his mind." That meant some powerful outside force had caused his condition, and women would tug their children and their pocketbooks a little closer to their chests when they passed him to be sure it did not rub off on them. They acted the same way when they passed the dark women in head scarves and gold hoops who handed out cards claiming that Madame So-and-So could work up a spell to get that curse off your money or find you a man, even if he belonged to somebody else. Some of the passersby tossed the cards in the street, but only after they were well out of the conjurer's sight. Others made sure no one was looking and then slipped the card in a pocket or purse for future reference, just in case.

Mama used to laugh about the folk medicines they used in the "olden days" before the young ones like her discovered the corner drugstore. Why would anybody rub ashes or salt on a sore to make it heal, she wondered, when you could buy a salve that would do the job just as well? You wouldn't catch her bothering to make a vinegar, salt, and garlic tonic to smear on the back of her neck for a headache when all she had to do was take a BC or Stanback powder. And nobody wore a bag of asafetida around the neck anymore to ward off disease, she swore, but you might dab some on your tonsils if you had a really bad cold. If she cut her finger in the kitchen she would not *think* of putting cobwebs on it to stop the bleeding; she would run for the Mercurochrome. But this is also the same woman who would call out to me "Don't kill it!" if I found a spider in the house, because that was a sign of prosperity. And if I slapped at my face like a deranged person as I tried to brush away the invisible strands of a spider web I had walked into, she would merely look bemused. "That's good luck," she would assure me, just as she had once been told.

They say that when the younger generations of Gullahs first started leaving their island homes for their new lives somewhere on the mainland, they were sent off with a piece of folded newspaper inside one shoe for good luck. Their folks knew how to make sure that some little remnant of the culture went with them, no matter where they finally ended up. The Gullah descendants I have read about live on the mainland, primarily near the coastal city of Charleston, South Carolina, and that stymies me, because judging by the atlas, the area where my grandparents

"Auntie" Mary Glover Williams, the family historian.

grew up is much farther inland. But based on the information I have been given, I figure I must be on the right track.

Every family has a historian, and ours was my grandfather's younger sister. She was an albino, with white, pasty skin and fiery hair. I have read that the Gullahs are noted for their dark chocolate skin and that mulattoes are a rarity. But this errant gene she inherited roams through our family, attacking alternate generations. (I was due, but I was spared.) As a result, our complexions have been diluted into yellow peaches and pecan browns, so I cannot go by appearances. Nature made up for its cruelty to my grandaunt, however, by giving her a fast mind and a clear memory into her seventies. "So, we're really Geechees, Auntie?" I asked her on the phone one day. Her laugh was throaty and mischievous. "Yes,

Grandfather "Bubba"
Charles Glover.

my dear," she began, slipping into her girlish proper voice that turned the last word into "dee-ear." Then the voice shifted suddenly into a sharper rhythm, confirming our heritage, "*We oneah dem.*"

On this trip, I carry in my purse a letter my grandaunt wrote me in shaky handwriting at my urging months before her death, recording the few family names, birth dates, and places she could remember. The note-sized baby blue pages with smeared ink are my only guidebook to Allendale. I've also brought along two photographs. Once more I pull them out, staring at each one as though the real story is hidden deep beneath the sepia tones. My grandfather's cat-brown eyes have a watery stare, like he is pained by something. Perhaps it is the uncharacteristic clothes—a suit and tie and wide-brimmed dress hat instead of the starched and ironed work shirt and cap I knew him to wear. It seems strange to imagine he had a life before me. He was the oldest of eight, not even twenty when he got fed up with farming sugarcane and cotton, threw down the harness, and left the Stoney Plantation and Stoney Pond behind. He went to work in a meatpacking plant in Jacksonville in 1922, I

Mama's mother Ruth McMillan Glover, circa 1930.

had learned from my aunt. The girl he had first married and took with him from another plantation was only fifteen at the time. I study her picture closely, trying to redefine the indelible creases that mar her dark, brooding face in the other photograph. The second wife had tried to crumble and destroy her image, but my mother retrieved it from the garbage. Wearing a dainty black hat and clutching an overcoat tightly to her chest, the young woman looks like a girl herself instead of a mother in her twenties. She seems shy and uncomfortable, like a country girl wearing ill-fitting city clothes.

From the moment I arrive in Allendale after the drive west from Charles-

Grandmother, Mama's
stepmother, Alma Glover.

ton, I am disconcerted. I expect to encounter curves winding up and down
steep country roads that dip like a roller coaster and spill into town.
Instead, I approach from a nondescript highway—not even an interstate.
The town consists of two stores, some houses, and a police station that
looks like a barn. The two-story brick complex I stand in front of looks
like an upscale apartment building, but it is a senior citizens' home. It
squats alone on one side of the street facing an empty field. The landscape of loss and desertion spotting the rest of the neighborhood looks
like the aftermath of a bombing in places, with only weeds and grass
where buildings once stood. Still, as I double-check the address of the
relatives I was advised to look up when I got here, I am relieved. It is the
first place I have located with any certainty.

After three rings of the bell, though, I am about to give up, when the
apartment door finally cracks open. I realize why it took so long. The
woman who answers and sizes me up warily walks stiffly and rests on a
cane. All I have is two sisters' names scribbled as an afterthought by the
grandaunt with the helpful memory. "I want to find out something about

my family in South Carolina, and Auntie says you're related in some way," I explain, holding out the paper as confirmation. The door swings open. I leave the mid-afternoon sun and enter a shaded living room where the silhouette of another woman beckons me over to the couch. She apologizes for not shaking my hand. "Arthur-ritis," she mispronounces it, "You understand." I am not even sure if they are related to me. These lanky, somber-faced women are half-sisters of my grandaunt's dead husband, the father of most of my cousins. They bear no resemblance to anyone on my side of the family, at least not that I can see once I adjust my eyes. But they are my late grandmother's first cousins, they say. The intricacies of southern family ties can be baffling. "Oh, yes," one of them says, "we knew her real well. We grew up together." The speech is flat and country, not patois, but the words are definitely hopeful.

I start firing questions. "What was she like?" "She was a pretty girl, real pretty," one says, and the other murmurs agreement. "Liked to have fun and wear hats." My mind does a quick flashback home to a closet shelf with my growing collection of head gear. I think about the young woman's somber expression in the photograph. I guess she was snapped at a sad moment or when she was having a bad day. "Did she work or did she stay home with Mama and her sisters?" I ask. They say they knew she had three baby girls after she moved from Allendale to Jacksonville, and one died, but that is all. "She died so young," one sister says, and they both shake their heads. I press on. "What did she die of?" Their plump prune faces wrinkle tighter. "Don't know. Something was wrong with her blood," says the talkative one with the cane. She could not for the life of her remember the name of the disease. Probably some type of cancer? I prod. "Her blood was bad is all we know." Maybe the city life got to my grandmother after all, I think, and she just pined away for home. Thanking the women, I head for the door, asking directions to some of the landmark places my grandaunt remembered. The Morrel Strange Plantation, where my grandmother grew up? Gone, they say. Stoney Pond and Moncks Corner, another place where they went to church? "Don't know it," they say in tandem. "We got the college up there near three-oh-one," the hostess with the cane suggests, eager to be more helpful.

The nearby campus of a state school looks as if it has been plunked down in Allendale as an afterthought, at the wrong moment in time, when everything else had gone. The main street, Highway 301, is barren. No more escapes for black people to the movie theater like there once was. No car lots. No bus station. The train route to Atlanta and New Orleans and north to New York still operates, but the train they called "the Southern" has shut down. No runs south to Jacksonville anymore.

Every town has a history buff, even if the title is not official. Ask around in Allendale and people give directions to the white lawyer who was born and raised there. He has helped a lot of African Americans research their roots, he says, and we talk awhile by phone. Quickly I become a captive audience to the friendliness of his rambling drawl. The rhythm of his voice is like swatting flies and hearing an aging back-porch storyteller liven up a dull summer night. He has heard of the old Allen African Methodist Episcopal chapel and cemetery where my relatives attended church and buried their dead. It is a mile and a half west of town, near a small stream—not a pond—on what was then the Stoney Plantation. At least *that* explains *something*. I always wondered why my grandfather held so firm to his Methodist Church affiliation while married to a staunch Baptist, although he attended early Sunday morning worship services only sporadically. Perhaps that was his homage to a past he never talked about. Moncks Corner existed, located halfway east to Charleston, one of the main ports where slaves were brought into America. For my folks, the first generation born free, this landmark was just one stop along a trail of planting and harvesting that led to the coast and down farther south to the sea island of Hilton Head, where the Stoneys also had property. Many inland folks lived a few months at a time on the coast, so contact between inlanders and islanders was not limited. Finally, an explanation for the Geechee connection. And whites and blacks migrated to Florida, especially Jacksonville, to get work in the phosphate business, the history buff tells me—that was familiar Geechee work. My people probably just followed other people they knew.

The last names of my late grandmother's family register with him: McMillans—lots of them around; Walkers—prominent landowners, not many left. He asks for my grandfather's last name. *Glover,* I tell him, and excitement raises the pitch of his voice a little. "That's a famous name around here, prominent in the low country," he says. I perk up, ready with pen and notebook to jot down the name of some surviving family notable in town who might tell me more about the branch of the family that stayed. But no such luck. There was a Glover who was a Revolutionary War colonel from nearby, he explains. There is even a statue of him forty-five miles away. Not many Glovers left, but it is a well-known name. My guide takes off on a tangent, one of those meandering routes that the puzzle pieces of history can take. He begins to detail some of the white military man's exploits. But the connection that fires him up only douses my enthusiasm; the surname imposed by a slave owner carries no badge of honor to someone who was that person's slave. I steer him back to the subject of Stoney Plantation.

The lawyer tells me about the owners of the plantation from whom my grandfather fled for the city. A man by the name of Stoney was mayor of Charleston for a long time. "Your folks," he offers, "come from very prominent people." Telling me that some members of the former slave owners' family were still in town, he suggests that perhaps I would like to talk to them to learn more. I consider it for a moment but reject the idea. Their stories would be mostly about the farmhouse lineage, and I want to know about the farmhands, who were probably just anonymous workers lost to them. The pieces would be just too odd to fit together. I put away my notebook, and when the storyteller takes a pause, I know I have heard enough. Minding my manners, I say, "Thank you much" and excuse myself. As I say goodbye to Allendale, I understand a little better why my ancestors made their exodus. There was nothing to keep them there.

I have a friend from Kenya who still maintains close ties to his African roots. Once I commented to him that I had a tendency to get lost trying to find a new address but could usually backtrack without a problem. "Black people can always find their way back home," he said simply, with conviction. For some reason, as I make good time driving back to the train station in Charleston, his pronouncement pops into my mind.

On the train ride home to Fort Lauderdale, I flip through some of the material from the Charleston tourism office on the Gullah, or Geechee, culture. A lengthy magazine article in the package catches my eye. It was written in 1949, two years after I was born, by Samuel Gaillard Stoney, no doubt one of my newfound "relatives." As I read, I feel as though I am holding up a kaleidoscope to history and giving it a twist. The angles and patterns begin to change and some of the mystery clears. Gullahs were, Stoney writes, "a happy medium type and enjoyed a consequent popularity in the authorized slave trade. The planters here were as particular as are our immigration authorities about the sources of the people they were getting to work for them." They had the "cleanest limbs" and were "more docile than, say, a Mandingo, but they also had a mean streak that could make them vengeful and even murderous so enslavers had to watch out." To whites, the two Africans—the Mandingos and the Gullahs—were as different in type as Italians and Englishmen, or so Stoney asserts. When compared to other black Africans, the Gullahs came under far more harsh criticism. They were belittled as being unintelligent and having "a sort of coarse-grained mentality," and they "spoke with comfortable uncouthness the crude old dialect of the plantations," the lyrical patois we admire so much today. Their Methodism was disparaged by the Baptists as the religion of the common people and the slaves. Eventually, Stoney points out, "Geechee" became a term synonymous with one who is unsophisticated and "country," and the use of the word was guaranteed to produce laughter or provoke a fight. It hurts to read such maligning, but I begin to understand a little better the complicated emotions my mother must have felt. Who would not want to escape such negative intraracial characterizations? A line leaps out at me, though, and I have to smile, recalling our household life. Gullahs, says Stoney, were "superstitious and fearful people." Recalling some of my family's traditions, that's one connection definitely made.

Now that the native sea island culture is nearly extinct, it has taken on a remote, romantic charm. Efforts are being made by some blacks and whites to preserve and study it for historical interest. But I am looking for the past to tell me something more. How does a person brought up in one culture make the transition and adapt to another drastically different one, as I did, for example, coming of age with integration? What makes someone even attempt to cross racial and cultural barriers, much less succeed? If these are my people, what is it in them that created someone like me? I am about to give up on finding answers when I spot something—a few more words about the Gullah traditions. Actually, there is not just one Gullah people, another article states. Their traits are an amalgam of those of numerous tribes from the coastal countries of Senegal down to Sierra Leone and Liberia—like so many coarse and fine threads intertwined over generations. I search my memory hard as I try to detect a few traces of those traits in me. They are barely visible at first, maybe, but slowly I begin to see. They are in the food, blended into the rice I used to eat, smothered with greens or okra and tomatoes; the fresh-caught, hard-fried fish with bones; the hot peppers, chopped and sprinkled or pressed into a sauce and poured from a bottle over everything that was not sweet. They are in the plaintive songs my mother taught me that sometimes swayed our bodies to and fro like the ocean in a rhythmic recall of the sad voyage that brought us over. They are in the stories told on the front porches and street corners where I lived, stories that began long ago around the campfires along Africa's west coast. Even then the language pulsated with a diversity of voices, sometimes friendly, some-times at war: Wolof, Mandinka, Limba, and Sus mixed with Congo, Angola, and Calabar. The white "buckra's" ways were just another stranger's spice added later to the multiethnic mix. And maybe long ago, certain members of the culture took on or were actually given the role of traveling from tribe to tribe to collect these disparate threads and weave them together, again and again. My mind echoes with what one of the elderly sisters said as I was leaving their home in Allendale. As the front door opened and sunlight fanned across my face and the living room, her eyes bored into me for a few seconds and she nodded. "*You one-ah we.*"

The train drops me off exactly where I started, at the station in Fort Lauderdale, and I feel lost again for a moment, disoriented here. Some people prefer familiar places to traveling, but there are others, like me, who seem to be wired for wandering. Even the logistics of travel are fascinating. I love stuffing disposable toiletries into a purse-sized plastic bag that expands and hangs from a closet rod. I find it challenging to select a miniature wardrobe for all occasions. I even like hotels, because I can take this compact, portable version of home there and get amenities without obligations. No apologies are necessary when I smear towels with lipstick, leave the bed unmade, and run the shower at 3:00 A.M. Nobody complains that I left too soon or stayed too long. For some people it is not the rigors of leaving that are frustrating, it is the inevi-table demands of returning, when they have to unpack and restore order again. When a trip is over for me, however, I enjoy observing the way life falls back into place. The toothbrush slides into the cup waiting empty on the sink. Hangers and shelves welcome the black dress, the red sweater, the suede shoes. The luggage is tucked out of sight but always handy enough to reach quickly when it is time to hit the road again. And some space can always be made for the new mementoes and the new memories.

My bags from this trip are unpacked and put away, but I am still sorting out my experiences. I know I traveled somewhere and came back with some new bits and pieces about the past, but I am still not sure how they all fit. Historical research can be peculiar, especially if the work does not turn up anything notable or scandalous, and especially when dealing with just plain old average folks. For years I have been digging hard and gasping for air; tunneling toward one relative and wandering off toward others on the periphery of my story; veering down some dead-end path and running out of information—or interest. Even if I do not know all their true names, I take some comfort in learning that I came from a family of immigrants—strange, resilient people isolated from others by their odd way of doing things and their peculiar views. I know that some migrated by force, like the Gullahs wrenched from Africa into slavery, and some by choice, like my grandparents, who left their familiar world to make a new life with the promise of better days. Others, like Mama, felt they had to forge new identities. And then there is me. I have followed the tradition of these strange people in my journey away from them and into the white world. I guess I am an immigrant, too. Maybe there is a spirit wind of those ancestral travelers who once ventured out to other tribes to weave those coarse and fine threads of color together. And maybe it stirred up again in me. At the sight of some new threads, I was lured far away from home on this journey, but I would have to learn how to weave on my own.

MAMA SAYS

*T*he two-year-old wears a ruffled sundress that drapes daintily over her shoulders. A ribbonned braid juts out from her head like a pointed finger. This black-and-white closeup is the only photograph that exists of me between infancy and high school graduation. It is the only physical evidence I have that I was in fact not born full-figured and five-foot-three. Of course, my mother is quick to remind me, it is not the only childhood photo that was taken. The one at five months old with tight black curls and chipmunk cheeks is still around. The satiated look, like a "fat kitten," the family says, sparked the nickname that became my unofficial first name for life. I remember another photograph of me at nine months old that, sadly, has disappeared. I have been told that it had been an unseasonably warm fall day and that I was in a fitful mood. The photographer finally amused me by repeatedly throwing a fluffy stuffed animal on the floor. I am smiling broadly in the photo, but there are tears in the corners of my eyes. A studio pose, restless and somber on my father's knee at ten, is also missing. There may have been a few school pictures at awkward stages of adolescence, but they were lost over the years with our moves from place to place. People did not take pictures back in those days like they do now, Mama reminds me sternly. Who had the money? But regret cuts deep into her words.

Perhaps that is why I became the self-appointed keeper of the family memories, and a shamelessly indiscriminate one, too. I refuse to part with scrapbooks that are bound with rubber bands and Scotch tape and overflow with twenty years of pictures of an ex-husband, former in-laws, and their extended families. I have shots of my daughter and son as they grew up in the suburban streets and backyards of Fort Lauderdale, but not the pretty portraits; those were neatly assembled in albums for them to keep. Mine are the discarded homely babies with severed foreheads, disheveled clothing, and unlit faces. The photos may be embarrassing, but with each rescue I feel I have reclaimed a little history. I have had so little to hold onto as my life has changed.

I stare hard at the little girl in the sundress above the brief inscription, "Kitty, 2 yrs." But memory of her is elusive. She sits chin up, face aimed at some point far beyond the eye of that camera, smiling broadly. But I sense sadness in the round, black eyes. I imagine more of a story there. She must have developed an early awareness of the incongruous. And she also knew about rising to someone else's expectations. By that age, her parents were separating and she was destined to be with her mother, on the move, left with strangers, left alone. Nothing in her life would ever be permanent, and eventually, even the world she was born into would disappear.

I recall only snatches of that northern Florida life I was born into. Back-porch afternoons shelling field peas or snapping pole beans. Stealing figs from front-yard trees. Crushing mulberries through a white sock for a teacup of purple juice the kids passed around as wine. Listening to the Coasters and Jerry Butler on the Negro radio station in the daytime and Elvis Presley and Johnny Mathis on the white megastation when I was supposed to be asleep. Adventure shows on television were always a more interesting backdrop than cartoons while I did my homework in the afternoon, but my most secret fantasies were told to head shots cut out of *Photoplay* magazine and taped on a wall. Parading in front of my gallery of stars, I practiced knock-kneed walking in a fishtail evening gown like Lana Turner for the day when I would be in the movies or performing for an audience. In the real world, my single mother shopped

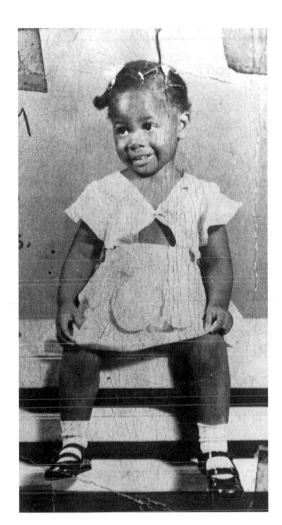

At two years old, 1950.

on five-dollar-a-week layaway at May Cohen's and Diana's, struggling to raise her only child in a two-parent community. Later I struggled to climb the black social ladder but never got near the top. I remember being shuttled from the projects to relatives to strange apartments. We were only in the projects for a year, Mama wants me to remember. And the stays with relatives and baby-sitters were short and came on and off. We do not talk about those very much; still, *my* memories were of a life that was unsettling.

But maybe that is precisely why it was so easy for me to leave in 1965, boarding a Greyhound bus for the newly integrated University of Florida at Gainesville in the central part of the state. "Cow Town," it was called, and the name seemed appropriate to this "big-city" Jacksonville girl. Leaving the homeland, looking for a fresh start in pioneer country, I entered white-dominated territory. That first term I remember glimpsing my image in the glass window of one of the classroom buildings; it took me a second to recognize myself. The navy skirt, baby blue blouse, and brown loafers looked a lot more comfortable on the sorority-girl types I saw bopping across campus with their shoulder-length haircuts swinging behind them. But the casual grunge of the sweatshirt and corduroys I had worn a few days earlier was not much better. I was sampling campus uniforms like new identities. My shadow darted out ahead of me, and I used it as a mirror, patting the curls in my hair to tame wayward strands and willing my back straight as I strode briskly toward classes that day. But I soon learned that the most noticeable thing about me would never again be my clothes, my deportment, or my hair.

The University of Florida had a student body of eighteen thousand. There were about thirty-five blacks total, including five black freshmen living on campus, that milestone year; I was one of them. Four years later when I graduated, there were about one hundred blacks. By then I was wearing tie-dyed clothes, singing folk-rock music, and hanging out with people who cooked Hungarian goulash and Indian curry and drank South American wine. Although I was in a minority, I discovered that being different can be very freeing. When some people find themselves in a foreign land—be it racial, cultural, or social—they react by retreating to a safe place among familiar faces, voices, and manners. Others turn defensive and fight for attention and space. But then there are those who try to fit in, often bruised in the process, as they encounter a new world. No one could have told that little girl in the photo just how far she would go, considering the stories she had heard about her meager beginnings.

The way Mama tells it, she was expecting to deliver me any moment when she woke up thirsty that night in early December and decided to brave the chill of the clapboard house to get a glass of water from the icebox. Slipping her arms into her flowered duster, she pulled the collar up close over her ears, careful not to snag the thin lace fringe with her wedding ring. The bulge in her stomach stretched. She paused and calmed it with a circular rub of comfort. Her face dimpled like soft brown dough as she smiled and eased her feet into the house shoes by the bed. Linoleum crackled under my mother's heavy footsteps as she walked down the dark hallway past the bedroom of her father and stepmother. Just inside the kitchen doorway she raised an arm to feel for the string dangling overhead and tugged it firmly. The room exploded with light from the bare bulb in the ceiling. Swiftly, something heavy and furry bounced across the tops of her feet, thudded to the floor, and clattered away like tapping fingernails. As the last inch of a long skinny tail disappeared into a hole in the baseboard, Mama, frightened, threw up her hands and screamed. As she tells this part of the story, her soft coal eyes swell with surprise, recreating the moment like it happened yesterday. "My heart jumped in my throat and I felt you jump in my stomach," she says. "You were nervous, too. See, we've always been close like that." And so it seemed.

I grew up fearing rats, all right, and so much more. A free-floating anxiety flowed through our household and not only kept our doors locked to strangers but also limited neighbors' visits. Beneath the veneer of tranquility in the old days, about which people wax nostalgically today, lurked a message that was programmed into me early: the world was not safe for a female child. I inherited a lot of things from Mama that I did not ask for and still cannot seem to get rid of—chafing thighs, a thinning hairline, and truck driver arms, to name a few. So, for many years, her explanation that genetics was also the root of some innate anxiety in my nature seemed plausible. Symptoms of this uneasiness had sprouted early. I sucked my thumb past puberty and gnawed my fingernails until they bled. During thunderstorms I hid under the bed. When clouds drifted by on a sunny day, I was the only kid who imagined fat, menacing faces. My perception was definitely skewed.

Mama had other stories to back up her claim about my overall tendency toward distress. I hated Halloween, she said, because when I was a toddler on my first trick-or-treat, we stepped off the stoop and bumped into a teenage neighbor in a witch's costume. The prankster startled me, and I cried so hysterically that we had to turn around and go back inside. I played with sparklers instead of fireworks on the Fourth of July because the loud noises jarred my nerves. I fretted and fought sleep when Mama got dressed up to go out at night, because I could not stand for us to be parted, she said, and she was the only one who knew how to soothe me. Humming in a honey-sweet alto voice, she fluffed her auburn curls and would watch me in the dresser mirror until I started to nod. Once she was absolutely certain that I was asleep, her lips would brush my cheek and she would leave the ceiling light on for comfort as she tiptoed out of the room. This aura of caution around us was magnified in the outside world. Even in public housing during the supposedly sedate late 1950s, the manual for survival included wariness. Our one-bedroom unit was on the second floor—safer from burglars, Mama theorized. Through one window she could keep an eye on the neighborhood; the other window faced the street. But she kept a .32 pistol in the bottom dresser drawer next to our bed, just in case.

I wonder now what private fears of her own Mama must have had to wrestle with late at night while I slept peacefully. She had married too young and married wrong, and now she was paying for it. But she was only in her early twenties, and she could still dream about being a housewife and giving me a home with a mom *and* a dad. Yet she woke up every day to a different reality, one in which she lived alone in a place she hated, with a school-aged child to raise and protect and a future she had to improvise day-to-day. She had generous helpings of mother-love and longing stored up, though—love she had once imagined she would get to share with four or five children. Instead, she poured all of it into me and I soaked it up, still longing for more. Occasionally she got off work early and picked me up from grade school before the final bell to go on one of our scheduled movie dates. I made short, fast steps to keep up with her as we headed for the bus stop, holding her hand tightly and feeling proud to have such a young, attractive mother. Soon after we slipped into the darkness of the theater, however, I would hear heavy breathing, deep and nasal. She was lost in sleep, but she had kept her promise to spend some special time with me.

She refused to get welfare like some of her friends, but still bought me play clothes, and church clothes, and two weeks' worth of school clothes every year. If she had an extra quarter, we shared a pint of black walnut ice cream; if she just had a nickel, we bought a dill pickle and took turns taking a bite. She would look at my puffy face and round belly in the mirror of a clothing store and tell me I was actually *cuter* because I was "a little heavy." And when she was not looking, I would sit on the bench in front of her dresser mirror and jab my finger deep into my right cheek, trying to force the skin into a dimple so that my smile would look just like hers.

At school, I was usually the last or next-to-last student left standing during the Friday spelling bees, and when I won, I got fried chicken, french fries, and sliced tomatoes that night for dinner instead of canned spaghetti. Once in third grade, the teacher sent a note home after one six-week period saying I would be retained if I did not improve in long division, and Mama, who rarely refused me anything, withheld bananas and Jell-O and slapped my fingers, so I knew this was serious. My homework was completed perfectly. If I pouted or answered her in a surly manner, her flash-flood temper would rise with every stroke of the leather belt that stung my bare legs until I cried. "I want you to know how to behave yourself and mind," she chided, "or nobody will want you around. You've got to know how to get along with people." I had learned to stop crying when she left me at a new baby-sitter's. What else did she mean? "You understand, baby?" I lied and said I did.

Sometimes she pulled out pans of clothing from the refrigerator and we would stay up late beneath the bare-bulb ceiling light in the kitchen as she ironed sadness into the pleats of my dresses. "You're so lucky to have a mother, a good mother," she once intoned, as if needing reassurance. "I never had a real mother to raise me." Dutifully, I replied, "Yes, Mama, I'm really lucky." Another time, sitting at the table beneath that same bare light, hands cradling her face, she cried. "Nobody loves me." I rubbed her back and cried too. "I love you, Mama." But she shook her head, "No, you don't. You're just going to leave someday." She loved me so close, as if she knew that time would soon run out for her to make her mark. "I just want to get you through high school," she often said. She had graduated; her parents and her husband had not. She wanted me to do at least as well as she had done. Beyond that, however, there was no future talk.

For awhile, I was content in her cocoon. It had plenty of books, neatly stacked in a corner of the bedroom we shared when I was not reading. They were arranged by size and subject matter—animals; cartoons; people; and Archie, Betty, and Veronica. Toys would slip into my life in December for birthdays and Christmases and back out of my life by spring. I watched dispassionately as the garbage truck carted away their remains.

"Cindy," with the brown skin and short curly hair, was the first black doll I ever owned; she was a novelty in the late 1950s. And "Blondie," her yellow-haired white counterpart, well, she had lasted the longest. The two slept on our bed during the day, took baths, and cuddled me to sleep at night. Despite several years of my mangling, they survived as my confidantes and playmates, with contorted arms and legs and plucked-chicken hair.

When I played outside, I had to stay away from the cluster of apartments where those "rough people" lived, the ones at the center of the neighborhood gossip. Miss A was having her fourth child from yet another father; Miss B sliced her old man's cheek from ear to ear the other night; Miss C's children went around begging and were always getting into trouble. I also had to stay within sight of our apartment door to make sure no one tried to break in—as if an eight-year-old armed with a skate key could stop an intruder. So I played Pitty-Pat and Here-We-Go-Zudeeo with the two girls across the courtyard who did not cut school and did not pick fights. They helped me steady myself as I learned to ride my new bike up and down the walkways without using the training wheels. But at sunset they had to go inside, and, "no, thank you, ma'am," I could not come in. Instead, I climbed on top of the toolbox on their back porch, and the rotting wood pinched my knees as I peered through the window screen at the scene inside. My playmates sat on the living-room floor in front of the television laughing, and I squinted, trying hard to make out the images they were seeing. But there was only a blur. I gave up and pretended to see what they saw so that I could at least laugh along with them. Mama says she saw me sitting there on the box one of those times looking in, and it broke her heart. One day, she came home early and called me upstairs. A tiny-screened black-and-white Sylvania sat on an end table in the living room, bought from a pawn shop and paid on every week. For a long time she took the bus or walked to work instead of hailing cabs. My surprise that day looked like gladness but it was not, at least not at first. The new television meant I was expected to stay inside even more now and would see less of my outside friends. In subtle ways I was already being sorted out socially, although I did not know it then.

I do not know exactly when I first realized that Mama and I had become separate entities. The idea just sprouted from bits and pieces of my own childhood memories and ripened with time. Somewhere along the way, the stories began to change; the texture and flavor of them were different, like new seasonings added to an old recipe. *She* was the one who almost had a heart attack when I lurched from behind the front door and shouted "Boo!" one day when she returned home from work. (I was punished with the warning never to frighten her again.) A damp smoldering firecracker had exploded in *her* ear and left her deaf for a few days one Fourth of July when she was a little girl. So, God forbid anything like that should happen to her only child. The anxiety button had been permanently installed.

Those of us who reached maturity with the women's movement in the 1970s set out to revise some of those tapes of limitation. Single or married, employed or at home, we tried playing the Super Woman role. We tested ourselves, challenged ourselves, proved ourselves. Those were the mantras. Now many of us, circling fifty, are feeling that nervousness and anxiety again. It is subtle, wafting into a conversation over cappuccino at a trendy café in downtown Fort Lauderdale as a jazz guitarist plays and tourists stroll by. Someone wisecracks that there is no need to rush home anymore, and talk turns to safety measures necessary now that you are a "mature" woman who will probably always live alone. It seeps out in a phone call with the mother of a young child during some moments stolen from her family. She brags about her precocious toddler, then sighs that her stamina is waning and that by the time he graduates from high school, she will be retired—and maybe single again, too.

I married and had children when I was young and stupid, I like to say, but I now realize that in my twenties I was seeking protection. While my single colleagues traveled for business and pleasure and moved around from job to job, I stayed anchored. Between romances, friends dropped by for our family potluck dinners, full of ambivalence about settling down, and I sometimes envied their independence. Two decades later, in their forties, some of those same friends turned desperate, seeking the family life they had missed, while I was the one who found herself ambivalently single. Now we are like diners at separate tables hungrily eyeing the other's plate. But many of us at this precarious new fifty-something stage are still trying to revise the old fearful tapes by testing, challenging, and proving ourselves in new ways.

A few years ago I began taking vacations alone—first around this country, then to big cities in Canada and Europe. It is similar to that bus ride

I took more than thirty years ago, except this time I have a better idea of where I am going. Anxiety oozed through the phone from Mama's voice to my psyche the first few times I told her of my travel plans. "It's not safe," she warned, "especially in times like these." When has it ever been safe? I wondered. But trip by trip she has become more of a cheerleader, passing on postcards and anecdotes to her friends, and they have become a cheering section, even if grudgingly.

Mama loves to tell the story of my birth. Usually it is recited when she calls to wish me happy birthday every year. I have revised it, however, to suit myself. The way I tell it, the reason I was born two weeks late is because I was so busy saying goodbye to my friends in heaven that I lost track of time. The nurse in the hospital delivery room had to summon me into this world by pounding a one-handed conga solo on my bottom—despite Mama's protests—because I had second thoughts about coming here. And when the umbilical cord was clamped and cut so that I could breathe on my own, some ties to Mama and her version of the world had to be severed, too. The reality of our lives in these later years is an undeclared truce in which my mother and I allow room for each other's view of the past. When we get together now, we tiptoe around more subtle things—the aging and the aged in a ritual dance.

I pull into the driveway with just an overnight bag for the weekend, counting the hours before I head out again. Two generations of my family have called this house "home," but I have never lived here. And I never will. Mama waves to me from the front door instead of the gate, and as I lean down to kiss her, I notice with impatience that her bowed legs are moving even slower since my last visit. Her litany of aches soon begins. After I eat I am drilled once again on the security system, the insurance policies, and the hiding places for her important papers. The adult in me struggles to pay attention while I swallow a surge of infantile rage. How I envy the people who have brothers and sisters. The odds are good that no one sibling will have to shoulder the parents' load alone. If some shrink from their responsibilities, others may take the lead. Only children, however, must dance to duty all alone.

Although I am passing middle age now, Mama and her friends still call me "the baby." I was the first grandchild and oldest cousin, now the family's reluctant elder-in-waiting. I have prided myself on being a maverick without a herd, experiencing life on my own. In the absence of

Mama and me.

comparison, I have competed with myself. On this visit, I wander around the house searching for the signposts of growing old instead of the mementoes from my youth. In the living room is an update of the beige-and-brown recliner that was one of the new pieces of furniture purchased by my grandparents when they first moved into the tiny three-bedroom stucco tract house after a lifetime of being renters. My grandfather used to sit in the first recliner, the guardian of two rebellious grandsons, barking out orders. He died much too young, before the age of seventy. In widowhood, my grandmother had more than a decade of spiritless decline as her legs weakened, her fingers became gnarled, and her eyesight dimmed. From that same recliner, she watched the last slivers of the outside world through the front door when someone opened it. Eventually she moved to the confines of a bed in a back bedroom that she never left. My mother moved in, quit work, and became her nurse. Over the years, the vinyl on the chair creased and the color faded. Mama threw a green cover over it.

And there she sat, with her eye on my grandmother's bedroom, looking for any stirs of movement in the hospital bed. And that is where she sat eating her dinner the night she heard the gasps that summoned her to my grandmother for the very last time.

When my children, now in their twenties, visit their grandmother, they regress to sibling squabbles over who will lounge on the comfortable roomy sofa closest to her chair. They keep her out past midnight visiting cousins and then sleep the next morning until ten. When I visit, Mama and I rise early, get home from errands by sundown, and like wallflowers, stay put for the rest of the evening unless some visitor calls. As always, I stretch out on the love seat a safe distance across from her in the recliner, and I nod fitfully after she gets up and goes to bed. Beside me is a case of shelves with photos I peruse with interest. Images of our family are there, of course, but so are those who are strangers to me. Little round-faced girls smile shyly beneath twisted braids and colored hair clamps. Little boys wear Sunday go-to-meeting suits and haircuts that make them look like miniature men. A serious-looking teenager stares back from a closeup; a young woman in a formal dress leans against a car. These are people I do not know—part of Mama's life, not mine. She has told me about them, she says, but I do not recall.

When she comes to see me, I often take out my scrapbooks, and we reminisce about her grandchildren's early years and the ex-husband and ex-in-laws and her younger days with them all. We flip quickly past the pages with scenes from my business and social activities and snapshots of people I call my sister- and brother-friends. Mouths are twisted. Shoulders slouch. Hair is awry. And most often my face is the only one that is brown. My mother says nothing, although she looks at me askance sometimes. But I see beyond what the camera sees.

MENFOLKS MATTERS

"**You**'ve got hair like your daddy," Mama often said. "Soft as tissue paper. All you have to do is dampen a brush with water and slide it on through." And sure enough, the curls unknotted like limber dancers and twirled into two ponytails. I primped in the mirror later, feeling for the hair lying flat now at the nape of my neck—we called it "the kitchen." And I actually believed that I was blessed to have a father who at least gave me "good" hair—until it curled up tightly again the next day. Sometimes the comb raked pain through the tangles. Mama poked, and I fidgeted, close to tears, which prompted her to sing. *Straigh-ten up and fly right.* "Your daddy used to sing that to me when we met," she would say. *Straigh-ten up and fli-i-i right.*

Soothed, I tried to picture him then, just turned twenty-one, a streetwise Central Florida farm boy, who had left home in his early teens. He was back from the war, waiting tables in Jacksonville and California-bound. As he swung through the door of the kitchen in his worn serge pants and cotton shirt, hoisting trays of leftovers from the diners—all of them white—she glanced over at him and flashed a dimpled smile. She was eighteen, washing dishes only because she had to, and desperate to get away from home. He brushed up close as he inched by her at the sink, fingering the top of her stocking garter through the white uniform. He liked to tease her about her big legs and her sassy walk. She wanted marriage. As music from the radio seeped through the clamor of the dinner rush, he leaned down close enough for his breath to brush her ear, and he crooned a popular song playing on the radio: Straigh-ten up and fli-i-i right. That New Year's Eve, they "flew" away together in a borrowed car to a town fifty miles away—Folkston, Georgia, where she was legal. After a brief ceremony performed by a justice of the peace, they sheepishly headed back home with no plans other than to be together for the rest of their lives. Although the marriage legally lasted thirty years, he stayed with my mother only twelve months—until I was born—then it was on and off until he flew off again somewhere, alone. Straigh-ten up and fli-i-i right, Mama would sing to me. I guess I got music from him, too.

However, it has taken me many years to acknowledge any real lasting connection. We always had such a distant third-person kind of relationship. "Daddy" was where I was sent to visit for occasional weekends, but his elderly aunts took care of me because he was always out with his friends. He scared me by driving fast with his hands off the steering wheel. Whenever I saw him, I was careful not to hug him too hard or too long, but most times I missed him once he was gone. His appearances at our apartment were unexpected, always brief, and often discordant. I knew to answer only his questions about school, never about any of Mama's business. And as soon as possible, I retreated to the television and turned it up loud as Mama shrieked about money and he stuttered rebuttals. When that stopped working, I created a new childhood ritual. I would close my eyes tightly and hum snatches of melodies, some I made up over time. I sang them over and over again like an incantation until I was numb to everything but the music as it spun a veil of sound around me. The visit usually ended with a slamming door, and so did my reverie.

By the time I entered my teens, Mama sometimes sent me on a back-door mission to summon him at the restaurant where he worked. I remember that narrow walkway leading from the corner of the building where Mama stood to the gray metal door I had to pound on for a response. The door opened just wide enough for eyes, a head popped out

Daddy's Song. Illustration by Janet Hamlin.

and nodded to the name I spoke, and the metal door closed again. Mama mentally telegraphed need as I waited. Daddy exited a few minutes later, smelling of onions and tobacco, and I reached up to tug awkwardly at his neck. A lighted Camel bobbed between his lips and my cheek. "Howyadoin', baby?" He spoke low and staccato, like he was already running out of words. As usual, the last word clung warm to my ears. Rarely did he call me by name. In fact, I was convinced that their marriage had failed because I had not been born a boy. But Mama swore that their "baby," at least, was wanted by both of them. Two emotions pulled at me on that sidewalk. I wanted to run back to Mama and tell her to do her own dirty work, but I had seen the last-resort look in her eyes as we climbed on the bus and headed downtown. And I wanted to run away from the curtain of disappointment that fell over his face when I gave him the speech I had rehearsed. *We need money*—the old familiar song. If I was lucky, he quickly dismissed me and we rushed our separate ways, heads down, empty-handed. If not, I stood there clutching the crumpled bills tightly in my hand while he stuttered in anger toward the face at the corner of the building. I waited until he was securely behind the metal door once again before I left. Either way, later at home, Mama hungrily quizzed me for every detail of the conversation. And that day was added to the chorus of complaints I grew up hearing about men.

Sometimes the words about men were whispered and giggled around kitchen tables with heads so close together I had to strain to hear. "Why don't you go on outside, baby," Mama urged, meaning sex talk was on the menu. And that was a subject that in my early teens was more taboo than my curiosity about Daddy. One day I asked, just asked mind you, out of intellectual curiosity, "When girls get pregnant, what bothers people more—the fact that they 'did it,' or the fact that they got caught?" Mama's temper caught fire with suspicions and severe warnings, and only after I reassured her that I had never . . . would never . . . did she calm down. But later that night, I held my pillow tightly to my lips and chest, practicing French kissing, pretending what I would do . . . when. But the men-talk could also be harsh and loud enough for me to know when the words were meant for my ears.

The woman who rang the bell one night had red eyes from crying. Mama offered her a beer, and her eyes reddened more. She had gotten into a fight with another woman, someone who was a friend at one time, over a boyfriend that they had discovered they were sharing. "I keep telling you, girl, you got to play them before they play you," said Mama, looking serious and firm in her feelings. She had some "mister-friends" but never allowed any of them to stay over. She said that it was because of me, but *I* wanted a live-in daddy. The visitor nodded. "I see what you mean now. It's not who you love—it's who loves you. I'm ready to be somebody's baby now and make them dance to *my* tune." She sniffed and pulled herself up higher in her chair. "A nigger's just no good. Can't trust 'em as far as you can see 'em." That word was sprinkled around often enough in my home for me to get the bitter taste. Sometimes the edge was blunted into something laughable, like a joke about someone who was too easily frightened or pitiably inept. More often, however, it was hurled in angry tones coupled with warnings to us girls. Beware of the older ones who lurked near the school yard jingling the change in their pockets and calling us sticky sweet names. Run home. Or beware of the ones who can leave you and bruise your heart. Usually somebody's daddy. I remember the first time I found out that a "nigger" could be me.

The city bus was pulling off that morning, and I ran so fast to catch it that I had to dig in my book bag for my student ID card after I boarded, holding up the line. The white driver did not try to hide the scowl behind his dark sunglasses as he waited. "Hurry up," he barked impatiently. The card was important. It allowed me to ride for a half-price fare on weekdays until I turned fourteen. And even though I was obviously a student, I knew that I was required to show proof. Finally I found the typewritten card, bent at one end like a dog-eared book but still legible. The bus shook as it idled, and the driver's razor laugh cut through me as I stood rooted there, trapped, while the others passed me, paid, and sat down. "You're too damn big to be thirteen." He was too loud. Shame trembled in my voice as I protested, "But I *am*." What else could I say? Still looking sideways at me, he stamped the card and took my change. Closing the door with a jerk, he accelerated. As I headed toward a seat, I heard him grumble beneath the exhaust noise, "You *niggers* are always trying to get away with something." I wanted to slam him over the head with my books. "He didn't know who he was talking to, Mama," I said, finishing the story for her that evening. I waited for her to flare up and "call a spade a spade," as she was known to do. I guess I pictured her dashing off to the bus company to complain. But she did not rage. She just shook her head with the saddest face I had ever seen. "Now, you can't let every little thing bother you," she chided, and my arms hung stiffly while she hugged me. If Daddy was around, I thought, he would know what to do. But he was not.

If mothers are daughters' mirrors, reflecting our similar or opposite natures, then good fathers are our buffers, smoothing our paths in life. When fathers leave us, the hole is palpable. We may try to fill it with lovers or sons or diminish it with self-reliance, yet there is always a melancholy underscore. I cannot say, however, that there were no men in my family—just not one who belonged exclusively to me. My grandfather came closest—the surrogate by default. Everyone called him by his last name, Glover, but when I came along, it got chewed up and drawled out into the toddler's version—"Bubba"—and that is the name that stuck. Even from a distance everything about this South Carolina man fascinated me. The applejack tobacco he chewed smelled like rotten fruit, but I was sure it was a wad of ambrosia from the way he cuddled it in his jaw. I tore off a chunk once and chewed it, thinking he would not notice. My stomach bounced up from my abdomen to my throat, and I left a trail of tobacco juice from his bedroom to the front porch. "Betcha that'll teach you, gal," he said brusquely, after my stomach settled again. Whenever he disappeared, I searched the house for him. The bathroom door was the only one he ever shut on me, and of course I wanted to know why. One day (I must have been about five) I stood on my tiptoes and pressed one eye close to the keyhole. The focus was blurry and hurried, but I could make out a side view of my grandfather's gray shirt and pants and could see that he was holding something; it looked like a long Baby Ruth candy bar. When liquid spouted out of it, my toes gave way and I ran back to the living room to wait, shaken from the forbidden escapade. That was the one place I never followed him again.

The starched and ironed blue-gray uniform and cap of a railroad man my grandfather wore to work five days a week must have seemed like a badge of respectability to him, second only to his 33rd degree Mason ring. He fussed over every crooked crease or loose button as though it was a personal affront. Perhaps he swallowed hard on life as a young widower in order to settle down again and gather his young daughters from relatives and make a new marriage and a home for them. He may have once aimed high in his mind. But the opportunities were limited for a black man in search of security, not just a factory or kitchen job. He could have shipped out for months at a time as a longshoreman or hit the road as a long-distance truck driver. Instead, my grandfather had one of the few jobs with a retirement plan and stability that was open to blacks. The Geechee had made good in the city. Several train lines crisscrossed the country hauling people or freight. So for thirty years, until he retired, my grandfather loaded ice onto railroad club cars at the downtown terminal. But from the way he talked, you would have thought he was an engineer. Rocking on the front porch and puffing on cigars with a railroad friend who lived upstairs in the apartment house and worked for a different line, the two men argued until nightfall about the speed of the Silver Meteor versus the Silver Star, like competing lovers. He spoke more words on one of those evenings than he did for the rest of the week. After his guest left, he turned gruff or fiery again.

My grandfather's second wife was a childless woman, tall and broad-shouldered with a stern, hawkish face, except when she smiled. Born and raised in West Florida, she plowed and harvested and never softened to life. In the big city she hand-waxed floors and lugged ten-gallon water jugs in office buildings, doing maintenance work at night until her body gave out. She retired soon after I was born and took me under her tutelage. Her only whimsies were the feathered church hats stacked in boxes on a closet shelf out of my reach and a foxtail stole left dangling from a hanger to try to scare me away from playing with her spike-heeled shoes. When I tried to take giant steps in them, they wobbled and turned over sideways like they were exhausted. So I marveled at how she walked about in them so confidently as she crossed the four busy lanes of traffic toward church. Every time the doors opened for a prayer meeting, choir rehearsal, Bible study, or usher board practice, she was there. She complained that there was no one to keep me and that she *had* to lug me along, but she spent an hour fussing over just the right outfit and hairdo to show me off. On weekend outings, I was allowed to follow her clomping footsteps through the grocery store with my short-legged running steps if I promised not to cause her any trouble about bedtime. To seal the pact, she bought me my favorites—chocolate and vanilla cookies shaped like diamonds, hearts, clubs, and spades. Most days I took some with me when, with the other neighborhood kids, I climbed the old oak that shaded the corner, swung on the moss, and ate warm figs from the trees that sprouted in the backyards.

At certain times of the month, my step-grandmother and I took the bus downtown to pay bills. I remember the panic I felt in one store when we were separated in the crowd. My head bobbed not much higher than a grown-up's knees. A flurry of calf-length dresses swept past me quickly, and every set of feet seemed to wear pumps or ankle-strapped heels. I did not think I would ever be able to pick out the sound of my step-grandmother's high-heels in the midst of that swirl of activity. We got back from downtown just in time for me to get washed, dressed, and ready at 4:30, when my grandfather trudged in. His usual gruffness turned gentle with me. "How ya doing, gal?" I waited until we were ensconced in front of the television to climb onto his lap for his attention. He cupped his face in one hand and closed his eyes as if he was nodding off. After a minute, he gently shoved me off, saying he was tired. I tried once more. "I got lost at the store today," the words spilled out. He was wide awake now. "I got lost looking for her, and the man in the store found me," I explained, getting more and more excited with the telling. "And they asked me who I belonged to, and I told them and they called her on the loudspeaker and she came over and I was so scared that you were gonna be mad and—" "What the hell?" He was calling out toward the kitchen to his wife. The bickering bounced back and forth between the two rooms. "If you lose her, you know *you* better not come home!" I beamed—until he shoved me away to her.

My step-grandmother was making magic on the countertop and stove just a few inches above my head. If I rushed to wash my hands, she promised, I could dust them with flour and squeeze the brown-sugar mixture through my fingers and massage it into balls. The twenty minutes that they stayed in the oven seemed like forever, but finally they came out as flattened cookies, and all for me. Perched on the little stool she gave me, which raised me up high enough to peek into the pots of mystery she was cooking, I had forgotten about everything else but the promising oven smell. As water filled the sink and the gooey pots and pans bobbed to the top, I made finger trails in the soapsuds. "You're such a big girl now," she said. "Here." A dish rag was slapped into my hand. But I got the feeling that this was no payoff—I was being punished.

Talk of Geechees and South Carolina had no place in the Florida wife's home. Instead, we talked about such small rural towns in the western part of the state as Live Oak and Marianna where step-grandmother had kin. But every Monday my grandfather paid a visit to his sister, my grandaunt, alone—probably to talk about the old Gullah days. When a weight of silence hung over the table at night, though, as often happened with two people of such different backgrounds as well as temperaments, I always knew how to get a conversation going. Just ask how some dish was prepared and I was guaranteed to get either my grandfather or his wife to dole out a few morsels of words that I could savor. Except for these precious moments with my grandfather, I had to borrow father-love from others. I became adept at inhaling secondhand the experiences of my friends who were self-proclaimed "daddy's girls." Fathers took them out to lunch or dinner for private moments. Fathers grilled the girls' dates to make sure their intentions were sincere. To me these women seemed to have a sense of confidence in themselves and an ease with men that I never felt. But I later learned that many felt stifled and unsure in life, that maybe there were pitfalls to being too daddy-dependent. Meanwhile, the estrangement with my own father took on a sad coat of hardening over the years.

When the word went out that high school kids were needed to picket a restaurant downtown, I signed up, and so did my friend Janice. At the last minute, she had to back out because her father was concerned that his city job would be threatened by her participation in the demonstration. But the risk was daring, so bold and exciting, and I was primed for teenage defiance. When the volunteers convened downtown at Hemming Park, we were handed signs and told to work half-hour shifts, walking in circles in front of the restaurant and chanting slogans to disrupt business inside. When the organizer pointed across the street to the targeted site, I swallowed hard. That familiar corner of the building. The rear sidewalk stretching to the gray metal door. Morrison's cafeteria. My father worked there. The longest half-hour I could remember stretched in front of me as I walked, keeping a stone face against the harsh glare of the occasional white patron who determinedly went in. One of them spit on the ground a few inches in front of me; my knees quivered, but I tried not to slow my stride. I was aware of being peered at through the sheer front curtains, by sympathetic black eyes, I hoped. Daddy was probably off that day, anyway; maybe he was even out of town again. Blessedly, my one-time-only shift finally ended.

I had no intention of telling Mama about this. None. And as time went by into my senior year, I forgot all except the relief I had felt when the afternoon was over. Several weeks after the picketing incident, however, I found out that Mama had asked my father to come by with money to pay for my college tuition. I had seen him only occasionally over the previous three or four years. But any hope of reconciliation was doused by the decibel level of their argument as they climbed the stairs. Mama's voice was sharp and distressed when she summoned me to him. I cringed, dreading what the outcome would be. *Did I picket Morrison's?* I shook my head. Avoid eye contact at all cost. *Someone saw you outside.* Traitors. *Didn't I know I could cost him his job?* The thought flashed by that Daddy had rarely spoken that many words at one time to me. I denied all but stood frozen with shame in the crossfire of his rage. The protective claws came out in Mama, who leaped to my defense, accusing him of evading the real purpose of his visit. Relieved, I watched as the tables turned again. In a calmer voice, but just as determined, he changed the subject and asked me about school. Surprised by his interest, I told him about my plans to attend the University of Florida. As I talked, he pulled out a crisp one-hundred-dollar bill from his frayed wallet. It was the first one I had ever seen. He tucked the wallet back into his hip pocket and, bypassing Mama, pointed the bill directly at me. A "but" was attached to his giving me the money. He wanted me to go to an obscure, small, black college in Alabama that a friend had recommended to him, and he promised to help out if I did. That would be better than taking the risk of going to a place where I was not wanted, according to him. Perhaps he had my welfare in mind and wanted me to have the education he longed for, although he had left school after the eighth grade. Perhaps this was his retribution for my protest act. But my future was at stake now, and I had gotten a glimpse of how different it could be. I balled up the bill and threw it at him and ran out of the room. That was the last time I ever saw him. It would be more than a decade, after I was married and the mother of two, before we even spoke again.

But he did leave something worthwhile behind. I still have a vivid memory of one Sunday morning, when I was about twelve, and I was visiting him. As the rest of my father's household got ready for church, along with his usual coffee-and-cigarette rebellion to religion he brought into the living room a new toy for me, he said. A record player, not monaural but stereo. He beckoned me to look at a stack of album covers and placed a couple of LPs gingerly on the record player's arm to drop and play. It was not music from church or the type of music played by the R&B station. For a few rare moments we listened together, eyes closed, to the raspy voices of Dinah Washington and Brook Benton curling around and teasing each other in a duet of jazz and blues. My father hummed along, and I felt he was encouraging me as I eagerly strained to pick up the words to these new songs of his.

Much later, it was music that introduced me to South Florida circa 1969, when people in the rest of the state considered the area foreign territory. The life of a struggling musician included late-night gigs on a then-decaying South Beach, hot-plate days in a then-funky South Beach hotel room off Twenty-third and Collins Avenue and thirty-five-cent matinee movies at the Cameo Theater. Music kept me in Fort Lauderdale writing about the nightlife of the entertainment-filled seventies and eight-

Performing in South Florida with Doug Adrianson and Ron Ishoy, in the band called Off the Record.

ies. In my youth, a guitarist with long spider fingers who caressed the slim neck of an acoustic Gibson wooed me, and for many years we played and sang together for our own entertainment. As an older woman, I have met other men who have used drums, guitars, and soulful lyrics to win my heart for short periods of time. But I most enjoyed singing solo around town just for fun. It might have been a stage at a charity affair, a dimly lit bar on an off night, or the corner of someone's elegant waterfront living room. And sometimes, when the melodies swirled and tickled and boosted all our spirits, I could almost forget that the white people at this party or this home would never invite me back there as a friend. Some gifts cannot be denied. At least that is true in my case. I guess you got traveling from your daddy, Mama says now, and the little girl quietly beams inside.

Mama was one of a few in her circle of women friends who actually had "papers" on her man. And in a strange way, the stamp and seal on the marriage certificate held. They stayed married for more than thirty years, until the day he died, living apart but becoming friends in the end. And time has brought some understanding to salve this daughter's scars. My father called me one day, after more than a decade of silence, to say that he was ill and that he loved me. We talked one more time before he died. He comes to Mama these days in her sleep more often than when he was alive, or so it seems. Whenever he shows up, all she says is that his appearance means it is going to rain. And more than likely, in a day or two, it does. If her father pays her an ethereal night visit, he is always laughing and in good humor—something she longed for but rarely saw in him on this side of the grave.

The faces of both these men sometimes surface in my slumber, too, at times when I am wrestling with a decision or in the midst of a life change. And their presence is as sweet and elusive as a lullaby. The tune is familiar until I try to hum it alone. My eyes open with a pleasant image, but I am left with no comforting words. Still, I notice that over the last year, some Dinah Washington and Brook Benton compact discs have crept into my collection. And some nights when the spirit moves me, I close the curtains, turn the music up loud, and just sing along and dance, and dance.

LEAVINGS OF HOME

"All aboard!" The announcer's voice boomed through the Greyhound bus station that August morning in 1965 as Mama and I settled into a corner of one of the long, wooden benches to wait. At our feet sat the three-piece set of red Samsonite luggage—her graduation gift to me for my first journey away from home. A few nights before, she had helped me empty the closet of the last of my winter clothes and tried to stuff them into the steamer trunk we shipped ahead to the University of Florida. But she gave up on her futile attempt at uncharacteristic neatness and went to bed. After she fell asleep, I packed again, carefully refolding the sweaters and jackets the way I wanted them. Mama had never traveled far from her birthplace of Jacksonville, and my trip would be to Gainesville, only ninety miles away. But I could feel the space between us widening as we sat still on the bench that day. "I just want you to be happy, baby," she said. "I will, Mama." My lines in the old childhood script were well-rehearsed. "Lord knows, I've done all that I can do." "I know you have; you've done a great job." She perked up, nodding her own reassurance. "Yes, I have. That's what everybody says." We were quiet for awhile, savoring the last of our together-ness. Then she broke the silence. "You know you can always come back home." I bristled at the thought. At seventeen, I knew I would never return.

Like so many of my generation, I had only leaving on my mind. We did not know where we were going or what we would encounter, but somewhere else sure looked better than where we were at the time. We were runners, plotting our escapes from the draft and Vietnam; from traditional marriages and nine-to-five jobs; from growing up, no matter how old we got. Sure, we launched some movements that transformed society, in spite of ourselves sometimes. But mostly we hitchhiked, crash-padded, and panhandled our way across the country or hid out in com-munes, cults, or colleges for as long as we could. Or we sought self-induced illusions with drugs. This is not the idealized version of our past that we tell our children, of course, or ourselves most of the time. We prefer to build statues of heroes and adventurers instead of shell-shocked, some-times misguided survivors. And the flight patterns of our generation have persisted.

Some of us have divorced so many times there should be a legal limit on issuing licenses. Others have delayed marriage or child rearing too long. We change businesses, careers, addresses, and relationships in a heartbeat, always with the ending in mind. This must have more to do with age than culture, since the attitude was not a part of my upbringing. In my experience, people had a tendency to stay rooted. Perhaps it goes back to the subliminal memories of the upheaval of slavery and its after-math. Leaving was considered a negative, unless you *had* to leave—for economic reasons, for example. The black community I grew up in was more a culture of gatherers. An "extended family" might consist not only of grandparents and stepparents but also of godmothers, play sis-ters and brothers, and other people's children as well as our own. And if some did slip away, the word was they were bound to fall on hard times and run back home.

Guilt tugged at me a little that August morning, trying to get in my way. "*All aboard!*" The announcement rattled off the upcoming depar-tures, including mine. Mama's voice trailed off as she stubbed out her third cigarette in less than an hour, her faraway eyes still focused on some memory. I was not listening anyway. I was on my feet, checking the time and double-checking my jacket pocket for reassurance that the ticket was still there. A white line bordered by the words "Colored Only" stretched across the length of the room, creating a small territory. Behind it, on other long, wooden benches, sat other black travelers. President Lyndon Baines Johnson had signed the Civil Rights Act in July 1964 desegregating public accommodations, but old habits died hard. I stepped across the line to get a better look at the clock on the front wall in the distance, then stepped back again, my heart racing with each advance of the second hand.

Finally. I tucked the makeup case under one arm and grabbed the handle of the largest suitcase at my knee. Mama rose more slowly, one hand lifting the last piece, the other reaching out for my arm as I rushed ahead. We kissed and hugged tightly before I climbed onto the bus. She tasted of menthol cigarettes and tears. The way Mama tells it, after the bus left, she joined some friends for a drink and then cried for days. "You held up better than me," she always says. "But I know it must have been hard on you, too, baby. After all, we'd never been separated." I sense the probing in her voice. Once I got to my Greyhound seat, I recall seeing her through the window, her image frozen as if it were in a frame. Her dimpled face held onto one last look and tried not to crumble. For a brief moment I wanted to call out—for a word of advice, for a description of what to expect. But this was my journey. As the bus rolled out of the station, the frame shifted and slowly inched away from her.

Each generation spawns its own retribution, I guess. We were runners, and we have produced children who want to nest. I have friends with adult children still living in the room they grew up in and borrowing money, while the parents are the ones who long to run away from home. We valued changes and choices; they seem to grasp for symbols of stability. Maybe that is why so many girls choose to become mothers much too young.

"*Write about me,*" my daughter says. Her voice on the phone has just a trace of the little girl whose antics I used to delight in sharing with readers in my newspaper columns. Despite her shyness outside her tight circle of friends, she basked in the attention she would get even from strangers who had read about her. In less than one decade, however, she went from a teenager at her junior prom to a single mother at twenty-one. And I became the bashful one about sharing her life with strangers. "*Write about how I'm raising my child and the things you taught me.*" I am caught off

With daughter Kali.

guard not at the boldness of her request, but at the resistance I feel. I still see her with the giggles, flashing her belly button and imagining herself as Hulk Hogan or Wonder Woman. Or sneaking and eating her younger brother's desserts at dinnertime when he was not looking.

She was an only child until the age of four, flirting with the camera that seemed to snap her image every time she smiled. She had cream-colored skin then—the bronze makeup would come much later—and summer would turn it to wheat and redden her cheeks. My favorite photos of my daughter are those of her at the age of five or six, sprouting a wiry, brown Afro fire-tinged by the sun; now her hair is dyed midnight black, close-cropped, slicked down. At home, she would scoot under tables and peek through pant legs like an imp to charm our mostly childless friends, and she acted so grown-up and demure when we took her out to nightclubs that we nicknamed her the "pygmy grandmother." In those days, our neighborhood was mostly white, and she was noticed, like an oddity. One little girl loved to bounce her hand on my daughter's bottle-brush of hair. Maybe that is why she always shudders when she sees her younger self wearing that look. She prefers the pictures from around age ten or so, when she wore twisted ponytails and braids cornrowed into concentric-circle designs. The neighborhood was largely black by then. Children used to call her names like "Red" and "Yella," I learned eventually, and they picked at her for having parents with darker skin.

But when the social worker first handed her over to me that Labor Day weekend in 1971, and I peeled back the cotton blanket, my novice hands quivered with excitement as those tiny pink fingers curled around my brown thumb. I felt such pride that the difficult part had been accomplished. I had grown up believing that it did not matter whether a child came into my arms through the birth canal or adoption, and now I knew it was so. This biracial baby was obviously different from me, too—born at a time when interracial relationships were still considered taboo, especially in the South. So she would be her own person, and I would have no expectations of her being like me. My generation was struggling with integration; children like her would bridge both worlds. We had it all figured out in those days. As my husband and I headed for our car that afternoon, curiously I froze at the top of the steps of the building. A wave of fear swelled up suddenly, unnerving me, and I would not walk down. I was certain that if I tried to take a step, she would slip from my arms and break apart, so he took her. She loves to hear that story. I do not tell her that the hesitancy has never completely gone away.

"*Write about how I'm raising my child,*" she says. On and off for weeks I try to untangle the feelings. I remember when I was seven. As I sat on the edge of the bed, struggling to keep my eyes wide open, my mother fluttered around the room in a whirlwind of motion, pulling on her uniform and lace-up shoes, laying out a dress and matching socks for me on the chair, and issuing orders. "Now remember what I told you," she said. "Make sure the top lock is on. And don't open the door for *anyone*." I thought I nodded. "You hear me?" This time I did. She peeled off the wax paper from my reward of pan-fried toast and scrambled eggs, with grits warming on the stove. Kissing my cheek, she headed down the stairs for the bus stop, calling out, "Take care of the house." After the door slammed, I scraped breakfast back under the wax paper and into the garbage, soaked the grits pot in the sink with hot water, and poured myself a bowl of corn flakes with two extra spoons of sugar. But I remembered Mama's mantra as I left home with my new necklace. I was the only student in my second-grade class who came dressed with a house key attached to a string around her neck.

At recess I was the one outside the circle while the rest of the girls sang: *Handkerchiefs-a-walking, walking-and-a-talking, handkerchiefs-a-walking, walking-and-a-talking.* They chanted, *Drip-it, drop-it, drip-it.* I dropped "it," the handkerchief, behind the back of one of the girls who was as fat as me but slower. She scrambled, grabbing for the back of my dress as I sped around the circle back to my space. I stuck out my tongue as she became the sulking outsider. Straightening my dress, I felt my neck for the string, but the house key was gone. The teacher dabbed at the puddles in my eyes as she tried to reassure me that it would be all right, but I was inconsolable as Mama was called at work. My fear strode through the doorway with her as she did a searchlight scan of the class-room that quickly landed on me. I cowered at my failure, knowing the trouble I had caused, but her words were a warm surprise of relief in my ear. "It's all right baby," she hugged. "All we've got is each other." And that is pretty much the way it was. I carried responsibility with me daily, but I still had my fantasies. I would have a husband and ten children—five girls and five boys—and I would never, ever leave them alone.

But even then my childish dreams of nesting were tainted by reality. At one point during those early elementary school years, I had to leave the house with Mama in the morning, and I was instructed to stop off at my aunt's to wait the extra hour so that I would have company for the walk. I would perch on the edge of the sofa and watch my six cousins, all younger, converge like ants for the breakfast feed. Stair-stepped in age, they lined both sides of the dining-room table as their mother lugged pots and spoons around the chairs and they barked out orders. And some tiny tyrant was sure to squeal for something missing or unwanted and set off wails that drowned out the television set. After a few times, I fled, convincing Mama that at seven I was a big girl and could wait at home safely, quietly on my own.

In later years, I watched as girls around me started to stake out their independence in other ways. In junior high it was Glenda, who sat two desks behind me. She had a baby in the eighth grade. We thought it was so sad that she had to get married and go to night school to get her diploma. By high school, a couple of other girls I knew only casually became mothers, dropped out, and disappeared. Nettie, I was close to. She lived in our neighborhood just a few blocks away, and we walked to school together sometimes. She lived with relatives—I think her parents had died—and she was the only girl my age I knew who had a job and paid rent. Her ample chest pushed tighter against her dresses, and she wore her hair flattened and waved instead of curled. Her boyfriend was in his twenties, and he gave her money. It seems strange now to say that for all those months through the end of junior year I watched but did not want to see. Her waist thickened, her blouses got looser, she walked with her books clutched against her chest all the time, and stopped dressing in gym clothes during physical education class. But I never asked her if she was pregnant. We talked about the same things as always. "When I graduate I'm going to New York to live with my cousin and work up there," she said. I said, "I just know I'm leaving here." There was a part of me that feared acknowledging her condition could make it contagious. I had seen the debris that could result. Nettie, however, worked, cared for her daughter, returned to classes, and graduated. But she never left town. The message was clear to me: single pregnancy could be fatal to dreams.

"*Write about . . . the things you taught me*," my daughter says. The grown-up who has usurped my little girl has no interest in my memories. A few feet from my computer where I sit trying to work, a painting hovers, large as a window, so I cannot escape the glare. It is a mixed-media canvas created by a Canadian friend who specializes in portraits of writers and artists that capture their "inner landscape," as a reviewer once said. I am swathed in bright, dramatic shades of rust and gold against a background of tropical Florida greenery. Posed like *The Thinker,* I look casual and carefree. Above one shoulder the painter has blended in a cluster of photographic closeups of my children as babies, done so deftly the technique is barely noticeable to some at first glance. The first time I saw the finished work, though, I was a little unnerved.

The women of my generation had worked so hard to break out of the maternal mode. Even those of us who did have children in our twenties found a way out trying to be Super Woman instead of just Mom. I scheduled day care, grocery shopping, and doctors' appointments between assignments and deadlines as a daily newspaper reporter and columnist. Weekends were booked with birthday parties, library visits, and amusement park excursions, looking for a sitter or praying for a sleepover. Then I would have a break so that I could slip into an evening gown for a night of work reviewing some entertainment event, or into slinky lingerie for a romantic evening at home when I just wanted to go to bed. I remember one harried Saturday afternoon trying to sandwich in doing a wash and dry load before a rare beauty salon appointment and running so late I was chastised by the hair stylist. Frustration fumed up inside of me. I used to get that way when I was little, my mother tells me, struggling to learn how to tie my own shoes. I fussed and cried that I wanted to toss the old oxfords away, but in the end I learned how to do it well enough to make it outside to play. As the stylist washed my hair, my tears cascaded down the drain with the soap. Once finished, however, I dried my eyes and headed out again. I have dealt with the uncertainties of motherhood in much the same way.

Now that I have gotten used to the portrait, I marvel at how the artist, then just a stranger, had sensed that side of me so quickly after only a couple of brief meetings. I wish I could meld the two images as well as he did. My daughter beams up at me from the painting's corner, a plump toddler who was then still balking when we tried to get her to walk. I remember how I sat cross-legged on the lawn that day, cradling her in my lap close to the ground. My son, in another snapshot, is perhaps nine months old. He was born after a long day of labor and was always small but wiry-strong for his age. The look is bemused, even blasé, as I playfully thrust him into the air naked after a bath. With him I do not seem hesitant or afraid. He was the second child, the younger and the last, the one I could not wait to see grow up so that I could get on with my life. When my son turned four, I taught him to make his own cereal-and-milk breakfast. When he was eleven, I got him his first paying job. My chil-

With son Brian.

dren both knew the plan—turn eighteen and it is time to leave, to be on your own. But for some reason it was easier letting go of him.

Sometimes now, when my son and I are out together and I sit across from him at a restaurant table, his long lashes will shutter his black eyes for a moment in vulnerability as the little boy creeps in. We might be talking about some of his antics as a kid or his big sister and their youthful sibling rivalries. It is the look a black mother treasures and keeps pocketed in her heart for those dreaded times when her son may no longer feel as open and safe. Other times, I see a shadow float across his face, and I want to ask him what pains and affronts to his manhood are buried beneath the grin he flashes at my worried stare. But I am grateful that he spares me. I do not really want to know. Instead, I wonder aloud when I last washed that shirt or where I bought that tie, only to be reminded that those are purchases he made. My son is just out of college and has been long on his own. Where did the oversized low-slung jeans, the T-shirts, and the faddish baby bottle nipples go? "Ah, Ma," he says, "that was the 'olden' days. Get with the new program." He called me over to

Kali, grandson Jordan, Brian, and Kitty Oliver.

his apartment one day recently to show me the new car he had bought without my help or advice: a sedan he had traded for his old two-door. He and his girlfriend are already planning a life together; many men in my generation are still "Peter Pans" and cannot commit to anything. My son is considering buying life insurance in his twenties, while I was in my forties before I did that. I just traded my four-door for a sporty coupe of the sort teenagers drive, and I "run the streets" with my friends to nightclubs and concerts, while he and his friends spend time "chilling" at home. We laugh about the generational shifts.

As mothers of adult sons we can content ourselves with occasionally being a buffer, soft arms against the brusque treatment of the world. Then we usher them back out there to stand on their own. Daughters we tend to hold close, for protection, we say. But maybe it is because we expect more from them in return. In a business gathering of her colleagues or in an apartment full of her friends, I watch my daughter move about without much reserve. She introduces them to her brown-skinned mother with a casualness that dares them to question, even if they wonder. She laughs silly at a joke. A man flirts, and she dismisses him slyly. People may look at her twice, speculating that she is Puerto Rican or Cuban, but she likes the attention, she says. In an all-black world she is most comfortable. Her dark-skinned brother, on the other hand, wearing proudly the burnt brown badge of his African heritage, moves more easily in the worlds of both races, but does so for business mostly.

Sometimes now, when I look at them both, I see such promise lost for my generation. The racial bridges we tried to build may never be completely crossed. But they have their journey, as I have mine. I remember that with my son, but I cannot let my daughter go so easily. Those fingers still hold tightly to my thumb. She stops by my home for a visit after her phone call and request. We cut corners in our conversation, telling only bits and pieces of what is happening in our lives. The times when I want to know more, I hesitate, biting my tongue on words of advice or blame. I want to pull her closer to me and make everything all right for her, but I fear my arms are never sturdy enough, and even if they were, I would just get in her way. We refocus our attention instead. With delight, I watch her little boy, Jordan, my first grandchild, diving off couches as Superman and autographing reams of crayon drawings, and I see some of her childhood impish ways in him. She begs her son for a kiss; he complies quickly, then pushes his mother away. The visit is short, as usual, but the sweetness will linger. "You may not like what I write," I say. *I don't care,* she says—kindly. And I know she means it. We hug goodbye and I watch their faces inch past in the car as they leave, but I have already rushed back inside.

TRIBAL WARS

I remember my first interracial encounter. I was sixteen and content to overeat and watch soap operas all day, when a girlfriend jogged me out of my routine to walk a few blocks to the nearby neighborhood recreation center. A notice on the bulletin board called for teenagers to sign up for various summer activities, including helping with a two-week black voter-registration drive sponsored by the national office of the YMCA. It sounded too much like work to me, but then we saw the clincher—some college students from out of state were coming in for the project. Boys! With a rush of adolescent urges, we scribbled our names and numbers on the sign-up sheet. A week later the call came, but my friend's parents would not let her go. So, reluctantly, I set out alone across the racial divide. This journey was peculiar to those of us who came of age with integration and racial change. We all experienced a memorable first cross-racial experience. Some of us were left wounded and discouraged as worlds painfully collided. Others found adventure as minds broadened and perspectives changed. It may have happened in a classroom, on a street corner, at a family gathering, or in a church pew, a desperate hour, or a lover's arms.

My maiden voyage began that morning at the sign-up table for the canvass. An elbow nudged my side, and a hand snatched my pen the second I finished writing my name. I grabbed quickly and snared one of the last large "Voter Registration" T-shirts left in the bin. Thank goodness for the commotion; at least I did not have time for second thoughts about why I was there. Twelve of us, mostly whites and a few blacks who looked a little older than me, boarded a van, and I squeezed into a seat between two white girls who chatted with each other past my head. I needed more space, but I was afraid to shift around too much because I did not want them to sense my feelings. The discomfort was there all right, but there was also the exciting sensation of being within breathing space of something so alien, so forbidden, yet so accessible. Once in awhile, one of them paused and looked down at me as if waiting for me to say something. I had no idea what. I pretended to look at the unfamiliar scenery going by. The van rolled down the miles of highway, then rocked along unpaved roads to a rural black area outside the city limits.

The woman with the sign-up sheet called out names in teams of three, and we each raised a hand to find our groups. I was disappointed when my riding partners disappeared without so much as a goodbye. A bolt of fear shot through me, a feeling that rooted me to the spot. What the heck was I doing out in the middle of nowhere? I might have remained there for the rest of the day if two new white faces had not rushed over. These new girls swooped me off down a narrow dirt path toward some houses. Sometimes a face lingered at the door, staring at the color contrast, I am sure, as I handed out leaflets and the other two talked. Sandy, a lanky senior from the University of Colorado nicknamed "the cowgirl," liked to hunch down close, her words loping along in her Denver twang like a slow, gravel horseback ride. "How y'all doin' today?" she would start. "Sure is a nice little place you got here. Whatya growin' out there in back?" The door would crack a little wider for her. Ellen was the passionate civil rights debater, her heavy, dark hair pulled back from her small china face like a kindly yet stern schoolmarm. She was from Oberlin College, junior year, majoring in social work. Shyly, I thrust leaflets into reluctant hands and smiled, feeling like an idiot. The first time I felt the warm hand of one of the girls on my back I flinched from the surprise of the tender touch. "Good job," she said casually as we continued on in the midday heat. Perhaps the experience would have been the same with any group of older people taking an interest in an impressionable teenager. But these were combative times. Life was cruel, we were told, and we had to be tough to survive in the white world we would enter. The battle lessons began as soon as we entered elementary school.

On Fridays, the two bullies in my fourth-grade class decided which girl would be selected as their "victim-of-the-week" and beaten up after school. The decision was not easy; there were at least twenty kids to get around to. And some of the tougher ones demanded rematches, which kept the bullies busy, leaving them only a few weeks until the end of the school year to play catchup. I stayed close to Miss Cromartie, the teacher, even wrangling an overnight stay with her one weekend, which meant we left school together, hoping to ward off what seemed to be the inevitable. This muscle flexing may not have been sanctioned by the school, but somehow none of the adults was ever around when it happened. It was a neighborhood rite of survival created not by outside forces but our own—a way of toughening us up for life, an inside course. Anger could be released with relative impunity, and a sense of power could be palpably exercised. The "winner" was supposed to show up after school at the designated spot for her painful prize and the chance to watch someone else suffer the same fate the next time around.

The grapevine sent a relay of signals across the classroom—a poke on the shoulder, a tap on the arm with a pencil, a kick against the desk—until it got my attention. I was the chosen one this week. Fear did a handspring in my stomach. The bell rang. Quick, I needed a plan. Miss Cromartie smiled sweetly at me, then headed off with her teacher friends while the students went their way. My book sack was heavy enough to swing like a catapult, but that would be like flashing red before bulls all heated up and ready to charge. As we filed out of the classroom, I imagined the thud of impact of a fist jamming into my stomach and the ache seeping outward like a puddle through my midsection. Maybe I would be lucky and just pass out. Muttering started behind me like a chorus warming up for the big finale. I knew a group of observers would be standing there to record every blow and look for the first sight of blood. I had no preparation for dealing with confrontation or this kind of random expression of rage. I needed daylight. Suddenly, I saw it: a side door off the main hallway that opened in another direction. I eased out quickly as the rest of the girls continued out to the yard, and I headed home a different way. At one point, panting and praying, I glanced back at the playground to see if I was being followed. To my surprise, the bullies and spectators were all still milling around, actually expecting me to show up and suffer as commanded. The next Monday, I was forgotten as they whispered a new victim's name. But avoidance was only a temporary solution.

A few years later in junior high, the self-appointed teacher was a tomboy band trumpeter who hung around the bathroom challenging girls to fight their way out the door. The day my turn came, my first choice of taking up permanent residence in a stall did not seem viable. "Go ahead and hit me," I said, resigned, as I walked up to her and swallowed hard. Her stomach punch sucked up all the air in my body as I coughed and tried not to gag. She waited, fist clenched and ready again, but I did not fight back, out of paralytic fear, not bravado. My mind had fled outside to the hallway and freedom, and I was praying that my body would soon follow it. A shield dropped over my outward emotions. She seemed surprised by my reaction and let me go. After that, she decided our conflict had made us friends, and I heard her brag to other girls at school about how I could "stand there and take it." But I could not understand why our people felt we had the right—the obligation, even—to assault one another just because the world outside could treat us even worse.

We had started to see the evidence of that mistreatment in the first half of the embattled 1960s, as the civil rights movement was escalating—and so were the clashes between blacks and whites. Reduced to a nine-inch television screen and sandwiched between afternoon cartoons and evening game shows, the scenes looked almost surrealistic. They were gruesome all right—demonstrators squashed by water from fire hoses and chased and beaten by cops and mobs. People lynched and assassinated. But still, this seemed far removed from my insular young world.

For instance, while many other churches around the South held rallies and became headquarters for organizing demonstrations, mine held meetings to warn the youth not to risk their futures by getting involved. It was before one of our special Sunday afternoon youth programs, as I dragged in sluggish and heavy-lidded from dinner, that the director of the department called the singers and ushers together for an "emergency" meeting. That was not unusual. We used to mimic this woman's big swaying hips and her deep, roaring voice that gave every pronouncement a sense of urgency. I figured this would be another chastisement about chewing gum or being on time, but her face was set even more seriously than usual. "As you probably know, one of our members has gotten in trouble with the police, and I just want to warn you all to watch out," she said. The murmuring started, and a name surfaced and shot around the room to me. He was someone much older, someone only vaguely familiar who had gone away to college. Still, I felt frightened for him. "If you get involved in that demonstrating mess, you can ruin your life. This boy is going to have a record, and he won't get back into college," she said. One of the choir members raised her hand and countered, "But I was told if you get arrested for fighting for our rights you don't get a record. They wipe it off." The director flared back, "Nobody in *my* department is going to have anything to do with this," silencing the girl. A few years later, after integration, the director was one of the first blacks to get a job in a white-owned dress store downtown. But that Sunday afternoon she echoed the belief of a vocal contingent of adults; the movement was for troublemakers, not people like us.

I replayed this verbal volley for awhile, not sure what it meant for me, but at sixteen I did not ponder it for too long. During the first half of that summer I had driver's education, anyway, a new course my high school was offering. President Johnson's new government program for the "disadvantaged" had been initiated that year and had provided the money for trailers with simulated driving screens and for two new cars. At least kids like me who saw no hope of ever getting a car could dream for a few minutes behind the wheel of a Volkswagen Beetle as we learned to back up and park. The social event of the season was a party to celebrate the end of the driver's ed course hosted by a neighborhood friend. He had a home with a carport, a portable record player, and the best collection of slow-drag songs. We organized a fund-raising drive to collect money for barbecue potato chips, onion dip, and Topp sodas, and we imitated line dances as if we were on *American Bandstand*. I cajoled my friend into rigging a round of spin-the-bottle. It was my first successful effort to beat out the competition, wrangling a shy kiss from the scrawny boy every girl in the group had a crush on.

But the sit-ins, and marches, and racial strife began seeping into my world more and more through the evening news. At home, my mind usually wandered as Mama watched the nightly reports. One day, however, as we sat on the couch with our dinner plates cradled on sections of newspaper, I became aware that I was paying attention, too. "Look at that child; she's not much older than you," Mama said. On the screen, a girl with a piece of her slip yanked down below her dress was trying to dig her heels in the floor as a policeman dragged her away from a lunch counter and into the street. She struck out, flailing, and missed her mark. "Good for her," Mama cheered, forgetting her food. "I couldn't do that—my temper's too short. No way I'd take that s———." "But why are they doing it?" I wanted to know. I could not picture throwing myself down on the ground and getting beaten up. I told Mama what the choir director had said. "Oh, some people always got something to say when you're trying to do right." She held me squarely in her gaze. "You just remember—right don't wrong *nobody*." I was not sure what she meant, but I began to listen more. And soon I became attuned to the sounds of strife. We could not avoid it.

A year earlier, when I was fifteen, an announcement from the school office one day had started out as a welcome break from the monotony of the classroom. We listened hopefully for word that a gas leak or a roofing problem had caused school to end before 3:30. At the very least, we could expect a quickly called assembly to meet a visiting celebrity, hear a motivational speaker, or cringe through a lecture on our cafeteria behavior. But instead, on that Friday afternoon in chemistry class in November 1963, our lives were changed when the announcement came that President John F. Kennedy had been shot, and then that he had died. School was dismissed, but few people rushed out. We froze in the hallways, sobbing on one another's shoulders that "they" had killed him and a part of us, too. After that, we learned how to stay braced for something ominous at any moment. And the familiar internal community squabbles and tensions started being eclipsed by "the movement" and more threatening outside forces fighting against change. We were taught how to set a formal dinner table and distinguish the fish fork from the sorbet spoon. We learned how to waltz, fox-trot, cha-cha, and square dance. In trigonometry class, lesson plans were put aside and we were introduced to income tax forms, preparing us to expect to make more

High school yearbook photo, 1965.

money than our parents. And then an announcement would come from that "other" world.

Once we were ordered to stay away from downtown because Woolworth's was being picketed because of the management's refusal to serve a demonstrator a plate of burger and fries. Police were arresting kids, even if they were just there to watch. Word spread that someone from our school had been beaten up by the cops and dragged off like some hoodlum, much to our chagrin. We had bragged that we had the best-behaved students in the community. Teachers with long careers who had been formidable role models were anxious about the school system's grudging plans to begin mandatory phased-in desegregation and the implications for their careers. Their adult insecurities stoked student discontent even more. Ironically, the assault from the outside caused the community, both blacks and whites, to coalesce into a troubled collective psyche. For us, rage turned inward with strange new stories of gore. A boy from my neighborhood was slashed in the stomach with an axe during a gang rumble and killed. The incident was so bizarre that it found its way into our conversations for weeks. The traditional rivalry between our high school and another one across town, once confined to the football field, escalated as quickly as the rumor mill. As anger traveled back and forth across town and stalked each campus with fists and knives, fights broke out, sometimes closing both schools. And television cameras seemed to be everywhere—at our school and all over the country—recording every instance of mayhem and confusion.

In a continuing 1964 drama in which we knew the good guys just could not win, one trio made an indelible impact on me. For six weeks I was glued to the television as the search went on to find Michael Schwerner, Andrew Goodman, and James Chaney, three young civil rights workers who had disappeared in Mississippi. On the August night that the special report bulletin interrupted programming to announce that their bodies had been found mangled and burned, I cried like a relative. Schwerner and Goodman were white; Chaney was black. The men had worked together and died together for one cause. For me, and no doubt others as well, they became symbolic of what the movement was all about. The villains were obvious—the white faces contorted with hate and distorted even more through the lens of the television camera. Like nightmares that stay vividly imprinted on one's eyelids after waking, the recurring images did not go away when I switched the channel. I could root for true bravado in the face of danger, even if I personally lacked it, as I watched society change on television. The time eventually came when I could even watch closeup, albeit vicariously.

It happened one day when I was on the Number 18 bus, probably on my usual ride home to the neighborhood after some downtown excursion. The driver maneuvered out of late afternoon traffic toward the three familiar-looking teenage black girls who waited at the curb. They were a couple of years older than me and had already graduated, but we had a history. They used to hang out near our high school and make fun of us underclassmen, who wore black-and-white saddle oxfords instead of pumps, and ribbons instead of barrettes in our hair. "Here comes the girl who looks like she's pregnant in the front and the back," they would catcall at me when boys were around. I started arriving for homeroom at the last bell, and I entered through a side door just to ward off that day's threats and mean-spiritedness. The teenage girls waiting for Number 18 now wore grown-up variations of the popular French roll and fluffed curly hairstyles, but I still cringed at the lingering scent of trouble. They shoved shopping bags from Diana's ahead of them, and their wide, gathered skirts rustled with starch and crinoline as they climbed up the stairs in single file to pay their fares. The first two cut their eyes past the empty seats at the front and headed to the back, sitting down in the seat directly behind me, snickering with mischief. I kept my eyes ahead and my antenna up.

The third girl's token bounced into the metal container and spun noisily like a top. I do not know what caused me to keep watching her. There was something about the way she just stood there for a moment longer than the others, surveying the seated passengers as the door closed and the bus grunted off again. Her mouth was set hard as her head swivelled and stopped, facing the long front seat with a side view of the driver. A white man, middle-aged and muscular in a white T-shirt, sat alone there, hugging the seat corner closest to the door. He braced himself with his right hand gripped around the metal pole. In the split second it took me to realize her intent, she spun around and sat down, a good foot away from the man. Cradling her shopping bag in her lap like armor close to her chest, she seemed to concentrate on some point beyond the window, behind the seat, and far past the white people facing her across the aisle. Not a word was said. The man swung his left hand around her back in a reflex action. His fingers clamped the nape of her neck, the way you reprimand a disobedient animal, and he shoved her forward—hard. She lurched off the bench, scrambling to stay upright and keep a hold on her bag. Straightening herself quickly, she swish-hipped toward the rear without looking back, her face emptied of defiance. She seemed to stoop a little, as if drained of air. The other blacks on the bus avoided looking her way. Number 18 squealed and slowed to another stop. Instead of sitting down, the girl nodded a signal to her two friends, who jumped up, and they all piled out in a rush.

"Troublemakers," muttered the older woman sitting next to me. Good, I thought. All those battle lessons did not help the girl much when she encountered a formidable foe in the outside world. But I could not deny her the brief moment of real heroism I also saw. Not the confrontation. It was when she stumbled and nearly fell but managed to regain her footing and keep on moving, past her anger and humiliation. Grudgingly, I felt a tinge of admiration. Few of us could remain on the sidelines forever with sign-up sheets at recreation centers and word-of-mouth fighting words nudging us on.

So in 1963, when I turned fifteen and a youth group of the League of

Women Voters sent out the call for some students to march in a protest down Main Street, I signed my name to the roster. We met in a church annex that morning to pick up our signs, placards denouncing the murder of Medgar Evers two months earlier. There were fewer than twenty of us, and the group was mostly older black women with sun hats and older men perspiring in suits and ties. A few of us young people were asked to fill in and bolster up the line of stalwarts. I watched as they each stepped off ahead of me, shirt collars already damp, legs bowed with time—braced for what? They could not be sure, but they took the risk. I felt a sudden rush of warmth for these people who could have been living rocking-chair lives and instead chose to fight for rights they probably would not even live to enjoy. But I would. I marched as instructed, a little steadier now—single file near the curb, eyes straight ahead, an ear out for trouble. The downtown traffic slowed to look. People stopped along the sidewalk as we straggled by. "What's going on?" asked one white woman barely loud enough for me to hear. "One of their leaders died, I think," someone answered in a hushed voice. A wave surged up in me, slow but sure, as I realized the force we wielded just by our presence that day.

I kept silent about the march for a few days before telling Mama. "You mad at me?" I was ready to be grounded for being so daring. But she surprised me. "As long as you're all right; that's the important thing," she said, and went back to stirring her liver-and-onion gravy. We sat down in front of the TV set with our dinner. Our hometown was on the national news. "Can you believe that mess? Look at that," Mama pointed. A group of bare-backed blacks in bathing suits jabbed it out with a white mob and police on the beach of St. Augustine, Florida. A wade-in led by Dr. Martin Luther King Jr. had turned into a bloody riot. The only thing I knew about St. Augustine was that it was the oldest city in the country. We had taken a class field trip there when I was in seventh grade. The teachers had warned us ahead of time that there was only one bathroom and water fountain for us, so of course all twenty-five kids had to use both. While we pushed and shoved for a turn, two whites-only fountains stood next to us, unused. One of the bigger boys broke the line and belligerently headed over to the empty fountain, but the teacher grabbed his arm and swung him around so fast he looked like a windup toy. All this happened in just a slow-motion minute as I was moving up in line. The big boy never did get his drink. That was his punishment. I hated St.

Augustine and vowed never to visit there again. "What's the big deal about that old beach, anyway? We've got two," I said. But since the black beaches were more than an hour's drive away, I only got to see the ocean once or twice a year for a church outing or when Mama had a friend with a car. "That one's closer," she said. "Should be ours, anyway." It would be thirty years before those pictures of strife faded, before I felt comfortable enough to break my vow and set foot in St. Augustine again.

Arriving amid such battles, the two young women I met so long ago at sixteen when we registered voters together offered me a respite for which I had been unprepared. In my first face-to-face encounter with white people, my guard eased down. In a way, Ellen and Sandy were the foremothers of the handful of white sister-friends who have become such an important part of my life today. We are fellow travelers who still must navigate around some deep divisions, who still must heal. As girlfriends, we still stumble along, learning how to share as openly about our racial experiences as our sexual rites of passage.

Ellen invited me to the party in the dormitory of the YMCA to celebrate the end of the summer's voter registration project. That night, a loose, soft cushion of hair clouded her face as she strummed her acoustic guitar, and the chords resonated with me. *Free-dom now. Free-dom now.* She sang to the tune of "Edelweiss," and her thin soprano voice blanketed the room. *I can see-ee it com-m-ming. Ev-very-where, if we dare, to stand and fi-ight for free-ee-dom. Seg-gre-ga-tion's a word of man . . . word of man, my brother. He's been wrong, but it won't be long 'til we all live to-geth-ther.* A warm feeling settled over me, and my back relaxed into the wall as I sat on the floor, listening. An arm stretched down from above to hand me a cup of soda. I glimpsed Sandy sprawled on one of the beds across the room, nodding with eyes closed. A black couple darting in and out of the adjacent doorway in animated conversation caught my eye. Like Sandy and Ellen, they were also college students, but I had not met them because they had not canvassed in our area. Yet I was transfixed as I watched how they traded jokes, exuding confidence, blending in. *E-qual-li-ty is a word of God . . . word of God, my bro-ther.* The young man strode into the room, careful of heads and hands. He gave Sandy a playful slap on the thigh as he passed her by. *We will live the word of God, when we all live to-geth-ther.* As the timbre of Ellen's voice rose with the final notes, the students stood up, linking arms and waists and rocking together. I joined them, humming along awkwardly.

My world did not change—at least not then. But I was aware of changes in the way I began to view the world. Once the routine of school resumed for my senior year of high school, I was outrightly battling some unsettling new realizations. In gym class one day, for instance, the teacher had that disgusted look on her face, like when she spotted dirty clothes on all-white inspection day. Frowns snaked across her face as she leaned over me on the tumbling mat, shouting instructions. "Head down, tight in your chest. Keep your hands wide and flat. That's right. Now . . . tuck and push. Over . . . over . . ." My knees rocked my rear end, which was hiked and frozen in the air. But nothing happened. "Next!" The teacher gave up and waved to the girl behind me in line. Still, I knelt there, head down, prostrate as if in prayer.

It had taken me three tries to make the minimum number of feet in the standing and running broad jumps. I was the last girl to cross the finish line of the quarter-mile run, winded most of the way. I managed to get airborne on the trampoline just enough for the knee drop, the sit-and-stand, and half of a twist-and-turn. Now, looming between me and graduation and escape from Jacksonville was the completion of a forward roll. The backward roll was no problem. I found that if I just sat down, clutched my knees, and fell back hard, momentum would somehow pull me through. Moving forward proved to be trickier. As I knelt there on the mat, I tried to picture how I had seen others do what seemed so hard for me. Their bodies curled gracefully inward as they relaxed, then tumbled like smoothly rolled dice, confident where they would land. I was less afraid of making the wrong move and breaking my neck than I was of being banished to the bleachers in defeat.

The "Miss-Its" waited in the bleachers in triumph. Those were the girls with good hair, whose bangs lay flat against their forehead without grease and who wore shoulder-length ponytails twisted like pretzels dangling down their backs. They were the pretty ones, because their light skin was tawny, amber, peach, or gold. Dark hairs curled above their white stretch socks and inched up their thighs to gym shorts that strained tight against their high bottoms. Their parents were doctors and teachers, funeral directors, shopkeepers—the social upper rung. One of them looked over at me sympathetically. She was one of several I had helped with homework at various times during our three high school years. I would have been a total "Miss-Out," but I performed well in the classroom. ("Those girls with light skin and long hair are dumb anyway," Mama consoled.) But I would have chucked it all to get an invitation to one of the Miss-It parties or, better yet, a second look from one of their boyfriends instead of some expression of pity.

Still, the importance of grades was growing. Passage of the Civil Rights Act of 1964 had laid out a new road map for blacks to get jobs in positions they had never held before—as clerks in the post office, inspectors with the city, tellers at the bank—but all that was still uncharted territory. The high school guidance counselors, who prided themselves in picking winners, continued to prepare us for one of two paths: industrial education or black college prep. I opted to apply only to out-of-state schools. Good grades were not the only social barometer, however. The "four-eyes" and "doofuses" socialized, but only in the science and math clubs. And athletes and majorettes were not voted most popular because of their grade point averages. We had a few oddballs, like the moody, dark-skinned boy who played violin and got a light-skinned Miss-It for a girlfriend, and the shy soprano, as thin as a sparrow, who sang lead in all our Gilbert and Sullivan operettas. And I was the writer who told stories and tried to ingratiate myself into upward mobility as a neighborhood Miss-It. My status, however, was always tenuous.

My mother was a single parent working low-paying restaurant jobs but determined that I would dress as if I blended. At home, however, she stressed different things. "Stay at home and stay out of trouble," she ordered. "I want you to be somebody," she nagged. "Don't run with the crowd or they'll run over you." Occasionally she would make the surprise announcement, "We're going to talk proper now." For a few minutes then we would imitate some perfect enunciation we had heard on television instead of the lax language of the streets. I had thought I was the one making her laugh that way, so pleased with herself, but now I think it must have been the irony of the situation. We were struggling to survive living in one of the roughest parts of the city and struggling just as hard not to sound or look like it.

The more alike people are, it seems, the more important appearances become. Beneath the veneer of community solidarity that has been painted over this period was a core of creative ways to tell "them" from "us." In our community, two people could live on the same street and pay the same rent but be given a different prognosis for the future. One would be considered a low-income street girl destined for failure, while the other was considered a prospective member of the middle class. What made the difference were certain rules: hang out with girls from the right families; take advanced science and honors English, not home economics or shop courses; and if you have sex, do not admit it—and whatever you do, do not get caught.

Chin jammed deeper into my chest, rear end hiked higher, hands pressed harder against the vinyl, I squeezed my eyes shut with resolve. A willful burst of motion propelled my thighs over my head. With a final push, I hurled myself forward and landed sideways with most of my body on the gym floor as my rag-doll legs slapped loudly on the mat. Awkward but adequate. The teacher shook her head as she handed me the sheet of paper with my name on it and another box completed with a check mark. The pounding in my temples gratefully muted the giggles as I walked away, light-headed. One of the gigglers took her turn. Her pale, slender legs flapped in the air unsuccessfully then sprawled gracelessly down again, landing in their original position. Still the gym teacher handed over the checklist with an encouraging pat on the back, and the girl proudly swish-hipped back over to her group. They had an air about them, something we Miss-Outs on the sidelines could only breathe in secondhand—a sense of entitlement.

That is what I thought then, anyway. Some females definitely had an edge over others in life. The illusion was fueled by my insecurity and the fear of being just a plain brown-skin-wrapped girl. But all of us Misses were on the same battleground, being prepared to charge into new territory where "they" were just waiting for "us" to slip and fall. If we ran in the halls at school, one of the deans told us to "stop acting like heathens" or we would never "be ready." For what, exactly, we were not told, but it sounded important enough for us to slow down. If a girl cursed out loud, she was sent to the office while the teacher reminded the rest of the class, "You see. That's why 'They' don't want us around." It was a compliment to be called a "lady." By contrast, acting "womanish" meant we were obnoxious and bold. Those of us urged to head for college were also expected to have children *and* careers. No wonder some black women who came of age with the women's movement felt like they were wearing ill-fitting shoes. Words like "strong" and "independent" became diatribes that could cost us the love of a man. Words like "pampered" and "pedestal" were sweet nothings many of us *wanted* to have whispered in our ears.

When I settled in South Florida and went to work as a journalist in the Fort Lauderdale area, there were few female reporters and no editors beyond the "women's pages." The first "Ms." to pump gas, drive a school bus, play a male sport, or head a city made the front page as a human interest feature. But being "the first black ———" was sometimes a bittersweet distinction, the subject would say, if she was also a woman in a white male world. During one of those story assignments, I ran into one of the Miss-Its from my past, now a noted educator in town, and I confessed my girlhood envy. She laughed. She had never thought of herself as a part of that group, much less among the privileged, she said. We struck up a camaraderie based on the mutual support system we members of the first generation of "new women" can uniquely provide for one another. No one had it easier, just different, we agreed.

My first extended encounters with white females after my experience at sixteen were on my dorm floor at the University of Florida. For the first two years, we were locked in together for curfew every night at midnight or 1:00 A.M. Illusions die swiftly when you see Merit Scholars sent home for academic failure and well-off girls with messed-up family lives. A special attraction of opposites drew me and Joan together. By that time I was a sophomore and one of only two blacks in that entire building. She was a freshman from Pompano Beach, Florida, and she was the whitest girl I had ever seen. In little ways I found myself toning down the contrast the more I tuned into her. Joan wore rouge on her pale pink skin. I started using blush on my natural brown shine. She wore rods all the time to keep her blonde hair curly; I straightened my hair with so many relaxers that some of it came out. One night, I even decided to learn how to shave my legs.

"No. Turn the razor over this way," Joan said, shifting the angle so that the end with the blade pointed toward my leg and away from the bathroom ceiling. She laughed, deep and throaty, tossing her hair back behind one ear. It was the first time I had seen a razor up close and in action instead of lying on my grandfather's sink, rarely used. There were no men living in the house with me and Mama, and none of the girls I had grown up with shaved. I wanted to become part of this dormitory bathroom ritual, but my patience was getting short. "Come on now, be serious. You've got to pay attention," Joan urged. "Shoot, black women don't *have* to shave their legs," I pouted. "There is always some man who is going to say, 'Hey baby, you sure do look good with your big old hairy legs.'" I kept raking the blade along my shin, the only place where there was even a hint of a follicle, and the razor kept gliding over that one reclining hair. Joan worked like she was mowing the back forty on one leg from her knee to her ankle, and she still had the thigh to shave. "A white guy would call you a gorilla," she said, stretching her leg across the rim of the sink and straining to get the area just below her buttocks. "They want it to feel smooth when they rub your legs." In the social-life department, Joan was queen of the floor. She sat in a yoga position as she talked to a string of boyfriends on the pay phone in the hallway. As the other girls walked by periodically and grimaced or pantomimed an obscenity, she just tossed her hair and dismissed the gestures with a playful shrug. When she had finished talking, she walked away trailing that scent her dorm mates had learned to recognize. Entitlement.

The reason for the limitations on my social life was obvious. I was black, and there were so few other blacks on campus. For the first time, it took the pressure off of me to try to compete in traditional ways. Explanations for the limitations of the white girls were harder to determine. I had to concede that the Miss-Its and the Miss-Outs had a much closer sisterhood than even I had imagined.

One night after classes, the general call went out to head to the restaurant across the street from campus for spaghetti and pizza. Joan and I passed. We were in her room painting our nails, concentrating on blending a new shade of polish from Pink Ostrich and Frosted Dove. "Do you remember when we first met, when I got here?" she asked. How could I forget? I had been her volunteer "big sister" pen pal over the summer and helped her get settled in the dorm when she arrived. "Well . . . ," she began. Her head stayed down and I could see a trace of brown in her yellow hair. "When I saw *you* were my big sister I said, 'Why me?' And when you asked me to go out to eat with you, I was embarrassed to do it." I stopped in mid-stroke, baffled. She was looking at me now. "But I don't feel that way now," she said, leaning over to touch my hand, careful of the fingers. "I'd go with you anywhere!" She paused, waiting for my response.

That night I got the first hint of some treacherous undertow in this new territory. A "them" and "us" within the sisterhood. I also realized that she was reaching out, attempting to span a racial gap she had felt between us, and she wanted me to commend her for her effort. I felt foolish. Because I saw no gap—or maybe I just did not want it to exist— I believed it was the same for her. Instinctively, I felt myself withdraw. In any moment of an encounter you have the choice to roll forward, however awkwardly. I managed the smile of acknowledgment she sought, and she relaxed, satisfied that our relationship had reached a new level of candor. I pulled back my hand and began rubbing off the damp polish with remover in swift, rough strokes, making sure this lesson sank in.

DOUBLE VISION

I am an hour early for a 9:00 A.M. committee meeting this cool spring morning, and the university and the town are already wide awake. Parking in the guest garage, I head out on foot to locate the right building for my appointment. Aging brick buildings I remember as dotting open spaces of lawn on Florida's largest campus are still standing, but they are now shoulder-to-shoulder with strange ones of concrete, metal, and glass that have been jammed in. Distracted, I do not notice until as if out of nowhere a tidal wave of white students arises and surges right into me. For a moment I freeze, and my alarm must show. One of the students glides up like an apparition and stops in front of me, blocking my way. I feel a quiver rise up in my throat, familiar as an old disturbing dream. In lieu of words, I thrust out my notepad with the scribbled address, braced for—what? I am not sure. Reading the words, the student tells me that I am standing right in front of the building where I need to be. He hovers so tall over me that I never get a look at his face before he disappears, but the voice is so mannerly he stops just short of calling me "ma'am." After a pause to recover and get my bearings, I am drawn off toward the narrow pedestrian streets, in another direction.

Revisiting old places always stirs up some nostalgia, but for black southerners in particular the experience can arouse pinpricks of pain. Remembering it all—the assaults on the spirit as well as the progress we have made—can sometimes be difficult. When those of us who were in that first wave of racial transition make our journeys back to the past, we are often like the walking wounded. Here I am, more than twenty years later, forcing myself to relive it again. *What was it like?* I know they will ask me that at the meeting, out of curiosity and deference to some relic who once helped integrate their campus. I will give them the distilled version, summed up, which says, "It was fun. I had no problems, really." And we will move on to the first item on the agenda. That will be the truth, too, or at least part of it. Considering the pioneers who got spat on, shot at, roughed up, or worse when they broke the color barrier—the solitary soldiers with just a movement's idealism to keep them company—my path was clearer. I like to say they kicked down the door and I was one of the first to see daylight and walk on in. The fine points will not matter much to the people I have come to meet. It is all ancient history in a way. I will not tell them that my memory is selective. Not the voluntary kind that turned young rock-and-rolling, antiestablishment hippies into the decency police, convinced that *this* generation is going to hell, nor the amusing slips of dotage we baby boomers now have that blur facts and erase names. In my recollections of that experience, the details of the disturbing dream are elusive, rushing by so quickly I have to strain sometimes to pin down images—a few minutes of fitful sleep that leave an impression lasting for days.

I remember how we first black freshmen held close to one another, maneuvering through foreign territory with the added baggage of first-year angst. One girl from our high school enrolled but stayed mostly to herself and eventually left; the other four of us set out adrift, hoping to find anchors somewhere. We were odd couplings. My "randomly selected" black roommate was a lanky, introverted, small-town girl from outside of Melbourne, Florida, where Cape Canaveral had just become Cape Kennedy. The two Mutt-and-Jeff–sized black guys, pals from Miami, played touch football with the dorm team and tested the social climate when Greek Rush Week came around. We were their dates at the dimly lit party room of the fraternity house that night. This was not so bad, "Roomie" and I decided. The sound system blared British invasion rock-and-roll, but once in awhile we heard a Motown song. Finally a taste of real college life. We guzzled the beer and solicitude from the members who already acted like long-lost brothers. But after the vote was taken a few days later, our guys got the word that they did not get in. Someone rich and influential in the alumni membership had vetoed their acceptance. "Whiteballed," I renamed it, which at least made us laugh. But the laughter was only momentary release from the bafflement and betrayal we felt. By the time we graduated, that fraternity made the national news as one of the first in Florida to integrate, but I had difficulty rejoicing at the progress. I knew about the egos that had been crushed while they struggled with change.

Slowly, each of us created our own raft. My roommate was the brain, the Merit Scholar finalist who buried her head in calculus and economics books and graduated early. She was destined to hit her mark in a high-powered, urban business career. Twenty years later, I found her number in an alumni directory and called, trying to reconnect. The greeting was warm, but the conversation was brief. The two guys from that night ended up finding their social life elsewhere, at black college campuses and back home in the big city. One of them earned his doctorate degree in psychiatry, I heard later from the other, a doctor of divinity. He and I kept in touch for awhile, but shared adversity does not necessarily create lasting community, and those faces are dim to me now.

As I walk across the campus, a sprawling brick complex sprouts up tall in front of me like a mirage. I go right up to the porch, through the double door, and across the lobby. No one stops me or even seems to notice as I try to wrench open the door to the first floor of this residence hall that had once been my home for two years. The door is locked. Back outside again, I circle the building to the side door, my eye on the window to the right, and I inch closer, trying to decide if I should peer in just for a moment. A young woman exits, and we are both startled. "I used to live in that room," I say, pointing, trying not to look like a common sneak. I know she is leery at first, but then she asks me if I want to come in. I shake my head no, remembering the many times I had waltzed out of that side door with expectations.

Once, when the notice for the campus theater group went up on the dorm's bulletin board, I decided to try out. In high school productions, I had usually been in the chorus, but I secretly longed for what I could never have back then: a lead role. My hopes rose as I entered the auditorium and saw the sparse turnout for the first meeting, even though I was a little late. The people milling around did not seem to be grouped in any way yet. A few of them huddled around the edge of the stage. I started to head up the aisle, aiming for a seat at about the midway point, when a male voice boomed out, "We're getting *all* kinds of people here tonight." His sneer resounded in the silence of the auditorium. Slinking into a chair near the back, I longed to disappear. I got drafted that night all right, consigned to work behind the scenes sewing costumes, and I quit before opening night. I resigned myself to being one of seventy singers in the university chorus and marking time until I could get home for Thanksgiving.

During the holiday, my old high school friend Janice, who was attending a small all-black Florida college, met me at our usual neighborhood corner as soon as we could get away from our parents. I could not wait to tell her all the things I had been too busy to write and to hear about her new life. It was instant recognition from the distance of half a block away, but the closer we came as we ran toward each other, the stranger she appeared. Her thin legs tottered in high-heeled pumps that matched her tailored suit with a dainty little bow at the waist. All she was missing was the gloves. I must have looked just as strange, my new blue jeans strained tight across my hips and my university's name emblazoned on a sweatshirt across my chest, as if I might forget. She talked about the creative antics she and her friends pulled to get out of the mandatory convocations. Her college, and many like it then, tried to use religion to glue the fractures surfacing in the black community. But the forces of change were too strong, and eventually the mandatory rule was rescinded. I had not even stepped into a Sunday morning service since I left home. The churches I attended had alternative methods of ministering to students: spaghetti dinner mixers, social protest plays and lectures, and presentations on Eastern philosophy and religious existentialism. A fledgling Reform Jewish congregation of politically active students tried to recruit me as a member and almost succeeded, mainly because the guys were cute.

One aspect of Janice's character had not changed; she was elbowing her way into a new crowd of Miss-Its, whose membership had expanded to include people from several states, with a lot more attitude. I leaned into a telephone pole, small and envious, as she regaled me with stories of the whist-playing, society-partying, dating-mating rituals she had enjoyed. I could feel myself slipping farther away. While I told her about some of my experiences, she listened, but with a question on her face. "Don't you feel weird there?" she asked, seeming genuinely concerned about my attending an integrated college. I just shrugged. How could I explain the waves of reactions that were sweeping over me?

Back at school, calls from home came every Sunday night to the phone booth in my dorm. "Are they treating you all right?" Mama would ask right off, her sensors turned on high. Her worry seeped through to my end of the receiver and hit a nerve. "I'm fine, Mama," I lied, waiting to hear the relief lighten her voice. She had no point of reference in her past for this new experience I was going through. And I had no words yet anyway for what I now realize was the shock and disorientation of being adrift in a new culture where all the rules had changed. In a lecture hall with two hundred students, I seemed to be the only one who was lost as a professor wearing a lavaliere microphone droned on about things I had never heard of in high school. The clinic doctor prescribed Darvon for the spastic grinding that had started in my colon and the migraine headaches that lasted for days at a time. After curfew and lights out in the dorm, the seniors on the floor introduced their fifths of bourbon and Southern Comfort, and I struck up an acquaintance that became too familiar and would cause me trouble in later years.

All that growing-up time with Mama practicing "talking proper" at home and being teased about it at school still did not quite make me acceptable. White people spoke differently. They used fancy dictionary words whose meanings I could only guess from the context, and I had to absorb a new vocabulary. It did not always come naturally, and sometimes I chose words that were imprecise or incorrect, as one of the "intellectual Nazis," as I called them, quickly pointed out. After years of being drilled by Mama to "speak up, girl," I became a whisperer. I got used to people saying, "Say what?" when I talked. Even my singing voice began to change. In the classical repertoires of the chorus, the choir, and the glee club I eventually joined, my warbling second soprano, which once led songs in church, was reclassified a second alto. I did not want to embarrass myself by singing high notes if I was unsure of a song's melody.

In the less demanding lower registers, my voice took on more confidence, but I was relieved that I could drop in and out among the others and sometimes even disappear. I rushed back through that dormitory side door many times to nurse my bruises, wondering if maybe the God I grew up with was punishing me now for striking out on my own.

Surely my salvation seemed to arrive the day a black worker with whom I had developed a nodding acquaintance took a break from gardening around one of my classroom buildings to make a suggestion as I passed. If my friends and I got bored, he knew a place where we could go. The magic word "jazz" spilled out, and I passed it along. Sophomore year was well under way, and two new black freshman girls had joined our tiny, loose clique. His news was music that lit up an otherwise dreary time. Someone was bound to suggest a Friday or Saturday night excursion by taxicab across the tracks to Sara's Jazz Club. It was not much of a nightspot. An uneven stairway led to a screened-in porch that looked like the front of several houses lining the street. Patrons walked up to the takeout counter where a man with a cigar sat on a bar stool doling out chips, pickles, and candy, and collecting dollar bills for entrance to the back room. If we were from the university, it was OK—gratefully, no ID required.

We were led to mismatched chairs at wooden tables that circled a dance floor in front of a tiny bandstand, and we sat inhaling rum and Cokes and fending off advances from men more than twice our age. Mama's old warning about the dangers of the streets back home replayed in my ear: "Whatever you do, don't go with an old man. They take advantage of young girls." Invariably she topped it off by cocking a wrist on one hip and bouncing to the rhythm of her delivery of the Moms Mabley line, "The only thing an old man can do for me is introduce me to a young man." One of the dangerous kind leaned over the bar, assessing us with a side glance. When he got enough gin down and enough courage up, he strode to our table in his shiny jacket and loosened tie with an outstretched hand. The straw in my drink became of particular interest, and I churned it around in the crunching ice as he finished nodding his way around the table with invitations to dance to a chorus of "no." We were smart college girls, hurling wisecracks at his back as he walked away empty-handed.

The best of the quartets and quintets as far as we were concerned played music we could at least snap our fingers to, our parents' music—blues and bebop, honky-tonk. No Motown or Aretha. Still, it was better than sitting at home doing nothing at all. "Don't I know you?" I recognized Darrell's voice, and the mocking tone gave me a familiar, excited chill. He had been a year ahead of me in high school, one of the "in" crowd. I was one of the outsiders who had a crush on him. I tried to sound casual as we chatted and he explained that he had just transferred to the university. I knew my luck was changing when I invited him to sit down and he pulled up a chair and even ordered another round of drinks for our table. He was starting classes the next term, he said. But his eyes darted around the club uncomfortably, as if he was looking for someone he knew or trying to see the person first. I did not dwell on the observation then, I was so flattered by his attention and his parting remarks. He wanted to see me during the winter break, and he asked for my number.

Two days after I got home, Darrell called. We went for a walk by the old school. In the shadows beside the front breezeway, he leaned me back against the brick wall. Later, in the movie theater, he stroked my thigh, and I was ready to spend my life with him. For the first time in months, since I had started college and entered a new world, I felt relaxed, a part of something, at ease. We rode down familiar streets past the storefronts and houses I knew so well from my youth, past the gold, bronze, and ebony faces strolling the sidewalks where integration would never make its mark. I snuggled closer to Darrell in the taxi as we left the theater, and I continued to be compliant for the rest of the night, even when I realized we were not heading for my home.

I started going to Sara's every weekend hoping Darrell would be there, since I had not heard from him and the new term was well under way. One night his best friend Mark came into the club. I could see him pause as if weighing a decision before accepting the invitation to leave the bar and join me at my table. Mark was bright and could have been handsome with his light curly hair and kind, cat eyes, but his face sagged sadly from too much drinking since our high school days. I bought him a scotch and asked hopefully if he had seen Darrell. His look was sadder than usual, pitying through his drunken haze. "Don't you know he's married? He's got a wife and kid here." The bottom fell out of my pride. When we had met at Sara's, Darrell was in town getting a house for his family, Mark said. Now they had moved down, he was in school, and his wife had started a job. I was just a brief interlude. I willed myself to sit there and finish my rum and Coke, but the pain barely left room for me to swallow. The other black freshmen, and probably everyone else in Sara's, must have known. I stumbled out of the club and hailed a cab back to the sanctuary of the dorm.

Curiously, when I arrived back home for my first and last summer vacation here, my social stock had suddenly risen. One of the Miss-Its threw a party at her parents' home, and I could not believe that I was actually invited. The hostess met me at the door with a hug and a high-pitched squeal of greeting as if I belonged. I strolled around the poolside, bouncing my head to the beat of the Four Tops cooing, *Sugar pie, honey bunch . . . can't help myself,* ready to soak up the atmosphere. The girls preened in lounge chairs, wearing bathing suits and hot-combed hair designed for posing, not for getting wet. I was overdressed, hiding my body beneath a miniskirt and blouse outfit I had made on a dorm sewing machine checked out at night when the other girls went out. It brought compliments from my friends at school but went unnoticed here. While they compared notes on the latest homecoming and fraternity balls at their black alma maters, I stood around cradling my ice cream sherbet punch cup and listening with an idiot smile.

The conversation turned to men—the ones they had dated or wanted to date. This guy was "lame," this one was "boss," that one "really fine." The assessment could be based on something as swift as a visual once-over sizing up a person of the opposite sex for suitability. The clothing had to look decent—a black man's style of dress was more important than his woman's. If he could be spruced up nicely, he could be taken anywhere. Skin color had to be considered, too. Some females adhered to the adage "If you're white, you're right; if you're black, stay back; if you're brown, stick around," and they color-coordinated their mates accordingly, with light at the top. The Black Power movement was on the horizon, but some sororities and clubs were still using the "blue vein test"—if the color of your veins showed through on the inside of your wrist, you were not too dark for a leadership role. Finally, the man's speech pattern had to be correct enough that it would not make your educated friends cringe. A split verb infinitive here or there was all right, but no "flat-talking" with dropped "g's" and "dem deres." If all that checked out, it was possible you had struck compatibility. If you had asked one of us in high school to map out our career plans, marriage might have slightly edged out graduating college. We had been taught that both options meant respectability and status in the eyes of the community. In fact, becoming a wife who did not *have* to work was a symbol of economic achievement and pride—even if just in fantasy—at a time, ironically, when white women were beginning to rebel against what they considered the marriage vise.

One of the girls summoned me over and patted a seat for me on the lounger next to her, signaling that it was my turn to share. "So tell us all about it. What's it like there?" she asked. I knew they did not want to know about the quality of the college education I was getting. "The pickings must really be slim." She tried to sound concerned. I drooped my head and nodded, conceding defeat. Perhaps it was the way they all shook their heads with such pity so quickly, but I got the feeling that the reason I was invited was to confirm that it was not any better—and perhaps even worse—at the integrated college where I had ventured. Their conversation headed off to other areas, away from me.

We read about the occasional female who moved into an all-male field, and we knew that new fields were opening to blacks, but we could not be sure of any opportunities outside of education, social services, or nursing—and mating. The pool of educated black males was small, and college was where you went fishing. In that respect, I realized for sure now that I was definitely *out* of the mainstream. Getting a man seemed to be even more important than keeping one, considering the way the women in the neighborhood sat around "playing the dozens" on the ones that got away. "Child, he was so ugly he hurt my feelings," one of them would start. *Girl, stop it.* "When he smiled, he had to strain so hard he looked like he was crying." *You know you wrong, now.* "He'd come home and get fresh and I'd say, 'Man, roll over and sing or something so I don't have to look at your face.'" The others laughed at the image to cover up their longing and regret.

In my household, the wedding ring was the ultimate symbol of achievement. Not that Mama wanted to marry me off—it was much more subtle than that. "I worry about you," she would say, with a forehead of frowns over the top of her glasses. "I hope you're meeting some *nice* people." The emphasis on "nice" telegraphed her suspicion, her worst fear, that I was being seduced away by these foreigners. But she also could not imagine how I could fend for myself alone without her protection, or someone's. I did not have the kind of rocking-chair women in my life who could spout homespun platitudes and offer safe harbor from life's storms. The women I knew were still wrestling with life. My step-grandmother wore her high heels and foxtail stole well into her sixties and cared more about her own social life than about any aspect of mine. My mother and her friends were still in the competition, arguing over who was better at attracting a man and the best way to "keep his nose open." But even they had begun agonizing over the frustrating changes in men, who were getting trickier to snare. A black man did not have to go to the back door hat-in-hand anymore, but neither did he have the front-door key.

In a field of nothing but white, on the other hand, I became the colorful exotic to be sampled. The first time a white guy I was attracted to cut his eye across the classroom at me and smiled, I flushed with surprise—and with pleasure. I liked the way his lashes fluttered low and suggestive, the way he teased me for hiding in the back of the room, the way he answered a question or made a joke and always looked around to make sure the conversation included me. We first clasped hands, then curled arms in late-night intimacies behind closed doors within that protected environment where we were suddenly set loose and free to experiment. There were others—soul kisses that never touched the heart. But my flirtations across racial lines, always hopeful, proved no more lasting for me than any others in those youthful times.

As I stroll around more of the university, I am lost for a moment. I encounter a maze of a new science center that has replaced the portables and frame houses I had once relied upon as markers to let me know I was nearing the outskirts of campus. But past a foyer I glimpse an intersection and traffic and I head that way. Across the street is something I do recognize—the row of churches and their student centers beckoning. Odd that they should appear now. But at this stage of my life, I have gotten used to these little friendly tugs at the spirit, as I call them—the messages that tell you to turn left, pick up the phone, or pay attention, that there is more operating in the world than what you can see.

The awareness must have stirred early, since my grandmother pushed me down the aisle and into the waiting arms of the pastor to join the Baptist church when I six years old. But *my* intentions then were less than noble. Even at that young age, I knew where I was headed: up front to sing. I first performed in the children's choir, with a very appreciative congregation. The choice of songs did not matter; applause was always enthusiastic, and we were cooed over for being so tiny and cute. No matter how bashful or forgetful we were, usually at least one of the two songs we sang had only one chorus, and we were always mercifully brief. As we got older, the stakes got higher and more competitive. We had to learn how to play to an audience while we sang for God. The congregation's limp-wristed pity claps were usually reserved for the unfortunate singers who took a very public fall. Those were the ones who stumbled on lyrics, warbled off-key, and never managed to right themselves: the deacon who would not admit he was now tone deaf; the aging soprano who insisted on hogging the floor; or the prepubescent child who whispered or mumbled or whose voice cracked and changed octaves with every note of the song. In the black church, music is such a serious endeavor it is no wonder so many of us go into show business. Whites may sit transfixed at all the fervor, the energetic displays of emotion, when they occasionally visit, but we are sizing up the competition. I had to work hard just to be second string, even at home. Mama was the real singer in the family.

I remember times when I was about ten or twelve when the weather warmed up and it turned too hot and stuffy inside, even with the fan. We pulled the sheets and spread off the bed and dragged them onto the front porch. With the lights off, the only distraction from the breeze was the beams from a car's headlights, arising and disappearing into the night. We sat there cross-legged on the pallet one night, me and Mama, sharing sips from a king-sized bottle of RC Cola. She stuck her thumb inside the neck and shook the bottle hard a couple of times, then unstopped it quickly and handed it over to me. "Bet you can't do it in three," she said. I loved this game. She started counting. *One.* I gulped the first swallow of foam and tilted the bottle down for more. The soda poured out faster, and it overflowed and dripped down the sides of my mouth onto my chin. *Two.* My stomach felt like a balloon about to burst, and the bubbles tickled and made me sneeze. But I held out, guzzling and swallowing and guzzling more, like she had shown me, until the final count. *Three.* Gas exploded out of my mouth. "Sounds like you're moving furniture," she deadpanned, then scooped me up for an underarm tickle as we wrestled on our makeshift bed. In the night, I could have been a baby again, trying to hold onto the playfulness.

The rollicking ended in a moment, like the closing of a shade that alters the lighting in a room. The humming and the slow rocking motion to her own music started. I stretched out on my back with my hands locked behind my head and listened as she sang out the trouble on her mind. *I know the Lord . . . surely will make a way. . . . Oh, yes, He will.* Tonight the trouble was money, which paid bills and bought clothes and food but never seemed to be around long. She had gone to work at thirteen; why couldn't I? But what would I do? Maybe I did not *have* to buy a hot lunch at school every day, although I would miss the hot dogs and fruit cups and spaghetti, and. . . . Activity down below the porch distracted me. From my pallet perch I could see through the railing as Mama's song surged. A couple walked by and looked up, but I knew they could not see us. Still, it was as if they were straining to do more than listen— as if they were trying to see the sound. *I know the Lord . . . surely will make a way. . . . Oh, yes-ss, He will.* She was worrying about something more, though. Perhaps she had hit a lonely streak again. The only "mister" around was our roomer, and he was old and had a girlfriend. But he brought home boiled shrimp and peanuts for us sometimes. *Although you may not have a friend . . . He'll be with you 'til the end. . . . I know the Lord . . . surely will make a way. . . . Oh, yes, He will.* The tears were welling up now. Oh, shoot; she wanted me to come over to her and get squeezed and wet. She was trying to fill up some empty spaces inside herself she could not tap into otherwise. "Sing with me, baby," she cooed. My tentative young soprano slipped in a half-step above her, then wobbled as I tried to hold onto the tail end of the notes she bellowed. Mama had one of those alto voices that rose deep from her chest and spilled out in full, round tones.

I had a "nice voice." But I wanted to be like some of those kid crooners who could milk emotion from a soulful repetitive phrase and elicit the loud "amens" and "hallelujahs" that would "tear up the church." Those were the voices that made grown men dab at the corners of their eyes with big white handkerchiefs, the voices that made prim and proper women collapse into holy spasms of shouting that tilted their organdy hats and brought out the smelling salts. Once I had moved up to the junior choir at thirteen, I finally got my moment. Boldly, I stepped up to the mike to belt out my first lead song. I sang out, *I'll let nothing . . . sepa-rate me . . . from the love-uv of God.* I sang like I actually believed it, and I did. The words swelled up and burst through my chest, out loud. For a few minutes I was transported somewhere outside my body, beyond them all, wonderfully lost in the sound. But as far as the director was concerned, I was the only one who held that feeling. My turn at the mike did not come again for another two or three years. It seems there was a bumper crop of musical child prodigies during my religious singing career. But music was not the only appeal of going to church.

In the outside, weekday world in which I lived, there were girls blessed with other attributes. They had much wider hips, rounder rears, sassier walks, and saucier attitudes. I was like wheat-colored bread for males who had light-toast-and butter-colored tastes. Sundays were my day of transformation. Church was also the one place a good girl could "court" with relative purity, and I experienced my first kiss on the lips at fourteen in the choir room after evening service. The thrill of summer Bible school was not just weaving a belt out of strands of colored rope. It was the tingle of a knee and lower thigh inching closer and closer to one of the older boys I had a crush on until we brushed together and nudged meaningfully before pulling away. In the sleepy shadows of a cramped bus ride home after a tiring evening performance, a hand squeezed my rear end through my robe. At least I thought it did, hoped it did, but I was not sure. Once I went away to college, however, I eagerly tossed off those family-enforced Sunday rituals for the secular life and its music. Preachers of self-reliance and rock and roll were much more mesmerizing.

But the same church I am standing in front of now lured me back in one day. I can still hear the laughter thundering through the open door of the Methodist Student Center, warming the chilly September night air as I explored the streets ringing my new campus home. I had stopped short on the sidewalk during my solitary stroll that evening and had looked in, curious. No pulpit, no stained-glass windows, at least not from what I could see. Still, for some reason I was drawn inside. A cozy area was set off with odd-colored sofas and soft-cushioned chairs and the casual clutter of newspapers, coffee cups, and ashtrays that had the look of frequent use. Three men huddled near the door with their backs to me; I could get only a glimpse of the fourth. His long fingers curled around the slim neck of a guitar in a spidery caress, while the other hand strummed its chest with washboard-sounding chords. The church music I was most familiar with did not sound anything like this. The beat was there, but soft, not pounding like a drum. And these three white men and the black guitar player were certainly no street corner doo-wopping harmonizers. At times, they sounded more like they were crying. But when they reverted to singing in unison, it was like sweetening in freshly squeezed lemonade. The song, I learned later, was the Kyrie, a Latin chant from Catholic mass. That night, I just closed my eyes and listened, absorbed. *Kyr-ri-ay ay-lay-ay-ay-ay-sohn,* they sang, lulling me with the music more than the words.

At the final whole note of the chorus, I came to and applauded. The singers broke rank and looked around, pleased. "Pretty song," I said, loud enough to catch the eye of the guitar player. He gestured with his head, and I followed his direction over to the couch. I did not rush, enjoying the feel of eyes that followed me with interest as I slumped down deep into a corner. A map of Africa was on his dark face, traced along the wide slope of his nostrils, the valleys beneath his cheekbones, and the arch of his eyebrows raised high and questioning. Some distant voices whispered of him in the masks and totems I had seen created by the inland tribes of long ago Mali. But I was intrigued by the music, and what it stirred up again in me.

In those days, my ears were more attuned to hearing people "spank" a piano, or pump a pipe organ to underscore a choir. The deacons "lined" hymns for a round of a capella singing by the congregation in what they called "meters," the tunes genetically encoded in us as far back as slavery and beyond. Gospel troubadours traveled the city and occasionally sang for a few scraps from our church's Sunday evening collection plate. They warbled to the accompaniment of electric "gittars" that buzzed and twanged so loudly we could barely hear the singers' words.

The guitar player said they were practicing for something new and controversial: a Sunday morning folk mass. He invited me to stop in sometime and sing with him. I did, hesitantly at first, and was introduced to the songs of the Peter, Paul, and Mary trinity. Then one day as we were playing around, he started picking out a stream of notes so touching I began to hum along instinctively, as if I knew them already. Snatches of

Singing at the Rathskeller on campus in the late 1960s.

the tune stayed with me for the rest of the day. Later, a little embarrassed, I tore a piece of paper from my notebook with some words I had written down and sang them a capella. He listened, eyebrows clinched in concentration. For hours we worked, refining the rough chords and softening the protest lyrics until they fit right into the arms of a new song. And he wrote a few songs, too, and sang them to me.

We went public for the first time on the stage of the Bent Card coffeehouse on open mike night. Fortunately, the dim table lights made the room so dark it masked my fumbled attempt to look casual as I hopped onto the stool and braced my feet to hide the trembling. We sang, *If I had a ham-mer, I'd ham-mer in the morn-ing, I'd ham-mer in the eve-ning all over this land*. My voice wavered a little as I loosened my hold on the last high note and held my breath, waiting. Only a few patrons dotted the room. They applauded, longer than necessary if they merely wanted to be polite, I thought. But I was wonderfully lost again in the feeling of the song. It was even better than church. The spotlight grew warmer, or maybe we just improved, adding blues rifts to more Peter, Paul, and Mary songs, tossing in a little "Stop in the Name of Love" Supremes number and Otis Redding's "Sitting on the Dock of the Bay" with a folksy, acoustic touch. If I was going to be the exotic, a curiosity, I might as well learn to enjoy the attention that at least lasted until the end of the set.

The music eventually led me into the stained-glass and pulpit area of the Methodist Student Center Chapel for our wedding the month after I turned twenty. It was a very public service. Mama stood up front in her green churchgoing suit, so full of emotion that she was sure to brim over with tears before I made it past her to the altar. Seated next to her were my grandparents—I did not remember ever having seen them go out anywhere together before. In that sea of white faces, like catching a fleck of color in the eye only when you look at it in a certain light, the three of them stood out as much I did. And yet, I had been absorbed.

When the doors of the church closed behind us after we said our vows, I could not have known how long it would be before I was lured back into the fold again. Or that we would be together for twenty years before the music finally ended. But now here I am, at midlife, scanning catalogs on retreats and pilgrimages and planning my Sundays around early morning services in a spiritual community I have chosen. What went wrong back then? My son, now an adult, was quick to point out the problem awhile ago, in that way our children have of making us feel guilty for ever thinking we were worthy enough to reproduce. How, he said, could we have failed to provide him with a religious upbringing since the rituals of religion are so popular with *his* generation? I tried to explain how in the arrogance we had had at his age, my generation figured God was dead. Our pursuit of enlightenment of other kinds, through drugs-sex-and-money lives, came at the expense of a traditional religious base, I conceded. But at least he was spared years of sheer soulless conformity. He did not look convinced. I guess sometimes people *do* miss what they did not have.

Perhaps that is why so many people in my stage of life are now embracing ancient and new age philosophies. Others are reassessing their religious roots. Prompted by an illness, recovery from addiction, a devastating loss, or a conscious reordering of priorities, we are flirting with spirituality—or chasing it outright—as hard as we once shoved it away. For some, the strings were always there, tugging at us no matter how much we tried to joke about it or tried to escape. To be black is to be particularly fated, it seems, despite assimilation into the white world. If nothing more, the guilt eventually gets to us. We grow up hearing sermons about the strong faith that helped the ancestors survive the unfathomable and about the restorative power of prayer to change hearts—and to change the world. We sing songs about death and resurrection that fill us with joy. Life is a journey of rough roads and dark valleys, we are reminded, so we become grateful for having a covered bridge to walk on when the hard rains fall.

The bell tower on the University of Florida campus calls out the top of the hour. I check my watch; it is almost time for the morning meeting, so I turn around. I must find my way back to where I started. With the building in sight, I walk with more assurance, following a path without paying much attention until I see the old cracked-and-chipped-paint remnants of Anderson Hall and I know I must go in. I climb the wide entrance stairway and, instinctively, another flight to the second floor. Boards creak and I try tiptoeing, although no one is in sight. Lights are on in the empty classroom I inch toward, the old-fashioned desks informally arranged. The window is propped open and the paint is peeling from its frame and sill. A desk with its back to the window sits there welcoming, but I hesitate. I know *she* is sitting there. I do not see her, but I sense her presence: a younger me, staring back from a place where I discovered her so long ago. This is the same room where I first argued about literature, read my short stories aloud, and received the news that I had been published in a literary magazine. Across the hall, in the office where the English department was once housed, I worked days typing letters, answering phones. At some point, I had felt the first stirring to become a teacher and the first realization that writing was God-given, and that no one could take that away. The floors are abandoned now, awaiting renovation, I am later told. I am glad I saw it before things changed forever.

By the time I graduated from that room, I was aware of the changes that had taken place in me. I remember the outdoor spring concert on the university's legendary football field, my last celebration with friends before leaving school. We had spread a green blanket on the field at the fifty-yard line, giving us a side view of the stage. Tie-dyed shirts dotted the festival crowd. I wore a beaded headband and a peace sign on a string of leather around my neck. As I stretched out on my back, the sun baked my cheeks through my round, yellow-tinted glasses. Someone nudged me and I turned over to get a refill of sangria. Sipping the luke-warm purple liquid soothed and numbed my throat as it went down and swam up to my head. Sighing, I leaned back again, propped up on my elbows, swaying to the whine of Santana's lovesick guitar.

The English department wanted an honors fraternity. When I agreed to help organize it, they made me the president. The campus newspaper needed correspondents, and on the staff was one of the fraternity guys I had met in my freshman year at the Rush Week party. He offered me freelance work, in part as an effort to make up for the embarrassing "whiteball" vote against my freshmen friends. More black students were enrolling, and even more should have been attending, so the university president set up a fact-finding committee on the "disadvantaged" and I was named chair. Somewhere in the midst of this whirlwind of activity, I began to find a way of weaving my own pattern from these strange new threads. I was discovering my voice as a writer and a niche on campus as a folk-rock singer. I had white friends now and a new black husband. I watched as, kneeling a few feet away, the long, thin fingers of his right hand flicked the imaginary strings of a guitar, his eyes clenched to block the outside world. He had created an interior life for himself that even I would rarely pierce. I was moving ahead. I felt a rush of comfort, a lull in rough waters, as the difficult journey started to get a little smoother. Some people derisively call this "assimilation." I had found a way to survive, if not totally blend. But crossings always come with a toll. I see it now in the schools with some of today's young teenage students, espe-cially blacks, who are supposed to reap the benefits of these decades of social change. The adventurers still suffer from the fallout of cross-cul-tural travel. Those who do not sit at the designated racial table run the risk of being shunned by their own. How well I remember.

Then, in 1969, as I was leaving the university, the black population was about one hundred undergraduates in a student body of twenty-five thousand. Blacks were being actively recruited now through a special program that gave them academic and financial assistance, but the pro-gram was not working very well. The white backlash charged reverse discrimination in admissions; the black reaction charged that not enough was being done to retain students once they arrived. Mixed messages beamed across the campus, as they did throughout the rest of society. We had our first blacks on the football team and as president of the student body. I was "tapped" that year for Mortar Board, a national women's honorary. The vote was secret but not the announcement. A group of women in robes made a candlelight march to my off-campus apartment to greet me on the front stoop and give me the news. But an anxiety fed by the type of insecurity that I find difficult to understand even today caused me to do something I would later regret. I did not know if I was being selected for myself and my worth, because I was black, or despite my color. In this atmosphere of change, where everything we once felt sure of now seemed in question, I doubted myself as much as I did the motives of others. I did not show up for the official ceremony a week later to get the honor I had earned. That would never happen again. Still, the people who are heralded as the "First Whatevers" wear their crowns uneasily.

As I walked around campus then, it was impossible to miss the almost daily fireworks. Sit-ins at the administration building for students' rights issues. Anti–Vietnam War petitions and nighttime vigils. Posters touting gay rights or women's consciousness-raising group meetings. Men in dashikis, doling out fliers to form a black student union. Where was all this when I needed it four years ago? Memories of the lonely, vulnerable feelings surged again as fresh as the first time.

Even the sudden rainstorm failed to dampen the mood of the concert crowd. We gathered the blankets and sangria and scrambled for cover. A couple hovering under what looked like a jumbo brown vinyl tablecloth waved for some of us to come over and join them. We giggled, taking off our wet sandals and brushing raindrops from our eyes as the muddy water of the football field lapped at our bare feet. The thermos passed from mouth to mouth. Someone found a dry match to light a joint and started it around the other way. It was the age of the flower child, the rebel, and the radical, the age of "tuning in" and "dropping out." We joked about joining fraternities and sororities. It was "in" to be involved, but not to belong. The rain subsided long enough for Sly and the Family Stone, the headliners, to come on and complete a set and one encore. Then, like weary players after a hard-fought game, the concertgoers straggled off the field and up through the stands to leave. Our group decided not to call it a night. I lagged behind, waiting for the couple who had offered us their vinyl tablecloth so I could invite them to join us. Standing still, scanning faces—mostly white, with an occasional brown—

I did not see a sign of them. Frustrated, I was about to give up. "Hey, sister. Come on and join us." The man's voice was close behind my ear. All I could see at first was a thin, dark forearm waving a piece of white paper I had seen before in front of my nose. I spun around, ready to say, "Sorry, brother. It's too late. I'm graduating in a couple of weeks." But words drained out of me. The face with the scraggly goatee, slash of mustache, and intense frown glaring at me was too familiar. It was Darrell. The flash of memories of the times at Sara's Jazz Club swirled back at me—the brief flirtation, the abrupt end, my unhappiness upon learning the truth.

I went numb. As I have done since childhood, the strategy of resistance took over. A shield dropped around me, and I became impenetrable. I could be seen, but I was untouchable from the outside, protected as long as I did not feel. I was vaguely aware that my breathing was shallow and that the face was steadily talking at me. "We're going to make some changes around here. The white man is not going to get away with mistreating us. We want what's due to us. Are you with us or against us?" His lips stopped. He looked down quizzically at the shield. "Well? Don't you have anything to say?" The shield looked back coldly. "I don't have anything to say to you," I snapped, and made an abrupt U-turn away from him. I was not prepared for the flash fire of hatred in his voice as I walked away. "Who the hell do you think you are, you goddamn half-white bitch?" The words were too harsh not to seep in, although I refused to look back for fear I would show my emotions. I walked faster as more of his epithets ricocheted against my back.

The volume faded once I left the stands and entered the concrete corridors leading out of the stadium. At that safe distance, I took a quick glance over my shoulder and saw him being calmed down by a couple of his friends who led him away toward another exit in the opposite direction. My legs were still moving, but quivering now. As I stopped and leaned against one of the pillars, the shield dropped and the adrenalin drained from my body. Once I got over the fright, I was baffled by Darrell's reaction to me. He acted as though he had been the one who had been wronged in some way. It took me awhile to sort it out, but I realized eventually that his resentment went beyond our personal relationship. His anger was more deep-seated.

We had both emigrated from an "Old World" that, for all its inequities, gave people a way of measuring status and self-esteem. We wanted to be pegged early as one of those students destined for more than just a diploma. Our first university choices were Florida A&M, Howard, or Fisk. But even if we had to attend smaller or less prestigious black colleges, we rushed a sorority or fraternity with the "appropriate" reputation, joining those who were the best looking, the smartest, or the most notorious party throwers. They became our network for friendships, for marriage, for jobs, for life. But integration, for all its appeal as a surer route to success, wiped out the traditional measurements. We were not only black now, you were a minority struggling to compete in the "New World." We were judged as a group while the group lay splintered in antagonistic camps.

For Darrell, discontent became a way of recreating a network, a new route to status and self-esteem. He had a small but vocal phalanx of like-minded friends around him; he also had the ear of whites who were frightened and fascinated by his rage. Sure, they feared the powder keg that was exploding into riots in cities around the country because of its destructive unpredictability. But beneath it all lay a bizarre dependency that still grips us today. Militant black voices are a war cry of anguish that whites understand because they, too, feel the need to strike out at something or someone to place blame for their personal pain. As long as there are people in both races *fighting* change, that is comforting. Others are suspect, if not the outright enemies.

At the sound of my name being called, I tensed up again. But it was my husband who had come back for me. His dark, somber face was lined with concern. The spidery fingers tapped my shoulder lightly. "Are you all right? I heard somebody yelling like a fool. What was that all about?" I wanted to tell him everything right then, to see him rush to my defense and protect me, to have him obliterate that face and others like it that I would encounter from then on. But he was powerless, and so was I, at least over other people. The best he could do was wrap a slender arm around me as I inched in closer and leaned my head against his chest. I tried hard to be content with just a momentary shelter. "It was nothing," I said, and I laughed—the kind of nervous sound you make when you do not want to cry for fear you will never stop. Over his shoulder I could see the young couple with the vinyl tablecloth quickly making their way toward us through the crowd. I have been finding *my* own way ever since.

As I weave through another rush of students, they seem to divide and glide past me. I set out for the committee meeting in the department's new offices, late now and prepared to make apologies. But I must organize my thoughts. I am scheduled to make a presentation about a scholarship for young minority writers to encourage them to give voice to their experiences. Although it is a scholarship I helped start, I'm not sure what I will tell them. I guess I could say that in a new environment, immigrants must often reinvent themselves to survive. I search for just the right words as I hurry on.

PART TWO

Incantation

to God for the path, and all the weary, wary, wonderful black, white,

and multicolored travelers I have met who remind me

I am not on this road alone.

—Kitty Oliver

JAMBALAYA

*T*he party was a Friday night dinner with some new college friends. "Nothing special. We'll just whip up a main dish we can all taste," the hosts said. People on their guest list came from places I had only heard of on television and in the movies, or had occasionally read about in books: Belgium, New Delhi, Caracas, Stockholm, as well as other parts of the United States. Most of the faces were new to me. We all had been instructed to bring something to share. I was almost twenty-one at the time, newly married, and the wedding ring my husband had slid on my finger was my badge of grownup status, or so I thought then. I already held a job, had a driver's license, and could have a baby if I wanted to. And now that I was a "Mrs." I could have as much sex and drink as much as I wanted— legally. But coupling also brought new demands. We saw less of our single friends, whose affections still roamed, and more of the friends who had been cut out of the herd by marriage or serious intentions. Instead of ordering takeout pizza and beer like we used to when we were dating, we scrimped on money and fixed thrifty home-cooked meals. But when we went out, it was usually to someone else's home where we did not just eat whatever was in the refrigerator at the time—we dined. I had to get used to a lot of things in this new social culture, like potluck dinner parties.

My husband and I had met the host, an engineering professor from Brussels, in the audience at the campus rathskeller where we were the local house performers. The man had introduced me to my first cappuccino. The taste reminded me of the little bit of the coffee with lots of cream I had been allowed some Sunday mornings as a child, when I sat on the back porch with my elderly grandaunts, dipping buttered toast into my cup until it was soggy and sweet. As I took my first sip of cappuccino, I lifted my pinky finger as I had seen actors do, almost dropping the plastic cup. The professor barely hid his amusement at that and at my lack of sophistication when I thought he was from the Belgian Congo. "Belgium," he corrected me kindly. His accented English was soft, like melting lard. I made a mental note to visit Belgium someday if the people were that forgiving. His wife was a third-generation Hungarian-American from Cleveland, a bookkeeper with a secretarial school education who grew up sturdy on hearty stews. Now she was taking French lessons and learning how to make dishes from other lands.

I knew that my specialties at that point—instant macaroni and cheese, broiled pork steaks, spaghetti with bottled meat sauce—would not be an appropriate contribution. Not special enough for this kind of gathering. My horizons were expanding with this circle, and I thought about the makeup of the group. An international garden. And I was just one of the varieties. So I brought flowers instead of food, and the colorful group welcomed me. I do not remember much about the specifics of the conversation that night or the many other nights that followed for a year or so. But I can still hear my unguarded laughter and the mix of accents as I sampled the centerpiece on the table: a dish new to me called jambalaya.

Now, understand, when it came to food, I thought we southerners knew it all. We finished our plates and scraped the pots clean. Even the act of cooking itself was considered an art second only to lovemaking. Instinctive. In our regional genes. Maybe that is why sex was often euphemistically sprinkled into the conversations I overheard as a kid. A cook could scrape leftover batter from the rim of a bowl with a finger and slowly lick it off to a chorus of dusky laughter. Or she could sashay her hips as she stirred a pot and purr, "That man can butter my bread anytime," eliciting knowing nods in response.

I, on the other hand, could never wash collard greens well enough to get rid of the dirty, gritty taste. My one attempt at cooking a fresh bunch of greens ended up in the garbage can along with the scorched cornbread that was runny inside. "Girl, you'd better get an education," Mama chided me. I did better at fried chicken, because it was easier to see the results of my efforts. I followed Mama's counseling to the letter, making sure the oil was hot enough, almost smoking, and that each piece was first pierced with a knife so that the meat would cook through to the bone. Some special seasoning was necessary—a little paprika—as well as time and careful attention. I remembered to turn each piece over and over again with a fork until it was juicy and well-done. For twenty minutes or so I was completely absorbed watching the white meat turn golden brown. I burned myself sometimes, though, if I stood too close trying to see exactly how and when the transformation took place.

I did not learn to pull myself away from the table fast enough, either. By the time I was twelve, we were shopping for my clothes in the "chubbettes" department, where dresses were size fourteen and above. But at home I was cooed over for being plump. So imagine my confusion when other people teased me unkindly whenever I waddled outside the door. The day our high school senior yearbook arrived and a friend pointed me out in the Honor Society photo, I still remember the shock I felt. At 180 pounds, I had mistaken myself for the girl standing next to me who was almost half my size. During my first defiant semester away from home at college in a competitive new all-white environment, I managed to drop thirty pounds, and I was determined to lose much more. Mama assessed me critically, however, as soon as I arrived for the holidays. "Your face is still nice and full, thank goodness, even though you are a little puny around the eyes," she decided. Only in my family was the loss of excess weight considered a problem instead of a solution. She fixed me a plate of oxtails, rice, and greens and piled on some cold potato salad, then proceeded to pick at my plate. "Why don't you get your own?" I whined, pulling the plate closer. "No, I don't want anything," she lied. "It just looks so good on your plate." By then her mouth was full and I was digging in, too, out of self-preservation.

In the South, we loved to eat; we even loved to talk about eating. But food meant more than daily sustenance. A hearty appetite symbolized good manners. A full refrigerator meant prosperity. With a dish in your hand you passed through anyone's front door. Breakfast was grits, not hash browns, and biscuits instead of toast. We ate liver or pork chops smothered tender in gravy as often as we ate scrambled eggs. Between meals, kids shelled pecans and drank Coke with peanuts that made salty foam when we put our thumb in the hole and shook the bottle hard. We might end up stuffed and getting sleepy-eyed, and the older folks might be "feeling poorly," but let someone come knocking on the door, and everyone perked up like Lazarus from the dead and the saliva flowed again. Something was always on the stove or in the icebox to put out for the welcomed visitor. And of course the guest could not eat alone.

Sometimes nowadays I get so discouraged about the minefields of hatred in this country that continue to lie in wait for those who dare to cross racial and ethnic lines. My heart can ache over an incident, especially in the New South, where so much movement forward has been made from so far back. Then I meet some other weary southern travelers—perhaps munching herring, meat patties, or frijoles—and we talk ourselves out of the misery and trouble by swapping tales about some of our more savory times when we were young.

In my neighborhood, we ate fresh turnips with the plump white roots, sweet mustards, boiled collards, stringed snap beans, and shelled peas cooked with the fat, knuckle, or muscle of a pig. We took tough cuts of beef and made them stew down and simmer long. Dinner was at one o'clock; supper was at six. We sipped "pot likker" from the vegetables, sopped up with a few slices of "light bread." Parties were crab boils with tables of old newspapers spread out as plates, and chicken and ribs grilled on a rack laid over a hole in the backyard. We southern children knew that mother's cooking was always supposed to be the best, but everybody else's deserved to at least be sampled. We were brought up to be good guests. We knew to smack our lips with appreciation, moan with delight after every other bite, and ask for two or three helpings of food. It was nothing to drop by a friendly home with just an appetite and expect to leave with a big bowl of leftovers.

Alone at our family table, we practiced peculiar social graces. As soon as I was big enough to sit there, I was taught how to mash clumps of fish caught by my grandfather between my thumb and fingers before I ate it to find any bones that might stick in my throat. A chunk of cornbread was nearby for me to chew quickly if I missed one, followed by a sip of milk to wash it down. Underneath the meat on the plate was white rice—always a dinner staple and bought in bulk, not by the pound. I do not remember being formally taught how to cook rice, but I learned that the key was to stir it during the simmering, but not too much because it was supposed to stay flaky and moist.

When my mother reestablished contact with a first cousin she had not seen in five decades, since her childhood, the relative traveled from her home in Washington, D.C., to Jacksonville for a weekend reunion. In fewer than eight hours after the cousin's arrival, the women had gone grocery shopping, cooked, and eaten three times. Over dessert they planned the menu for the next morning's breakfast. Even now, years later, they still reminisce in detail about the food they bought but did not eat. As I get older now, I bristle at my mother's reminder to "keep up your weight." "Thinness in old age makes you look sickly and underfed," she says. In rebellion, I keep my refrigerator and cupboards sparsely stocked with low-calorie, low-fat foods. But every so often when I feel in need of a respite, I sneak in some food for the soul. More than likely, however, what I have a taste for is something exotic.

That night in college when I tried jambalaya for the first time, I did not realize how much of an affinity I would develop for it. A door cracked open, and when I got a peek at new combinations beyond what I had been seeing, my eyes clung to the vision hungrily. As the party guests took turns spooning out portions, we shared poignant memories of our childhoods and other comfort foods we had enjoyed. The recollections were as sweet as the tender chunks of onion and as sharp as the aromatic assault of the garlic cloves. In the shadows cast by the candlelight, my friends' multicolored faces almost paled in contrast to the red swirls of tomato and the pink-tipped shrimp, the bold green peppers, the firm, pink strips of ham, and the brown, supple bacon. Aside from a little salt and pepper to taste, there was a pungent spice I could not identify. Thyme, the hostess said. She wrote out the recipe, and the one-dish jambalaya meal has been a part of my integrated life ever since.

Research has shown that migration tends to be selective. People who leave their familiar surroundings for another culture usually have an affinity for the culture to which they migrate. That may be true for me, because from the day our first black-and-white television set appeared in our living room when I was in elementary school, I began absorbing images of white people—people distinctly different from me. I watched pretty much whatever was on, but my favorite shows were the ones with complex figures. I had a preference for flamboyant swashbucklers from different cultures, like the heroes of *The Count of Monte Cristo* and later, *Zorro*. Zorro had a dual identity and baffled people, appearing to be a wimp one moment and performing heroic deeds the next, always eluding discovery. I also liked the offbeat cowboys who preferred talking to fighting. An early favorite was the title character of the program *Sugarfoot*, because he was bashful but had good intentions that ultimately won people over, even when his social graces were lacking. And *Maverick*'s star was a savvy gambler with a charming soft spot underneath, which he showed reluctantly. Although the crises of these programs changed from week to week, they were always resolved happily, and in the end, regardless of their shortcomings, the good guys always won. It was difficult to reconcile this neatly packaged fantasy world with my day-to-day reality. No one came to sell vacuum cleaners, encyclopedias, or other door-to-door items, but there was home delivery of the white newspaper and access to Avon products; both had black representatives who lived in the neighborhood.

The only white person who regularly visited our world was the man who sold life insurance to people who lived such a basic existence they could barely scrape together the payments week to week. On Saturday morning, he parked his car at a corner and walked the block with his bulging leather satchel tucked under his arm like protection. When he rang our bell, Mama made it clear that she believed in covering health, not life, and she said proudly, "I do my business at my job." So the phantom passed over our house for other doorsteps, hurrying along with his tie as crooked as his manners. "How y'all doing," he drawled, tipping his hat and addressing folks by their first name. He was always "Mister" to them. I never liked that, or the fact that the potential customers grinned and offered him a napkin and some lemonade to sit awhile. He was always trying to get into their business. "Them some good looking grands you got. Is that a new baby?" People thought he was concerned, but he was just curious. "Put that little one in a policy now and you'll have some money for him when he graduates high school," the insurance man urged. "And besides," his eyebrow arched pointedly, "you just never know what can happen to him between now and then." After he left, the family counted their fingers. The payoff would be only a tenth of what they would have to pay him. He had wheedled them out of additional money for another life policy because they did not dare risk the ultimate humiliation of appearing not to care about their loved ones. They wanted to be able to bury their kin in the unlikely case that was necessary, and a little windfall possibility tucked away for future years could be an incentive. More immediately, it was important to them that this white person, this outsider, think that they believed in taking care of their own.

On a rare occasion, one of my mother's white coworkers brought her home when she missed the bus, dropping her off just as quickly as the woman for whom she sometimes did day work. One of them might ring the bell and share a catch of fish or slip us a small loan, but the stop was brief and the acts furtive, as if they were betraying some code. That is how separate we were—antagonistic, suspicious, uneasy if not threatening. We met and sparred and returned quickly to our mutual corners. Even if I could imagine having more contact with whites than this, the prospect was somewhat fearful. Surely I would lose something, something would be taken away from me. My comfort level would definitely be disturbed. I would not know how to act, or what to say, or how to say it so that I did not sound dumb or be misunderstood. These whites were not real people like I was used to; these people had the power to disrupt, to destroy. This was the kind of one-dimensional unreality about the "other" that the absence of personal experience can create. The seeds of that change Mama was predicting had already started to sprout without my being aware of it. Yet in a relentless, insidious way, distorted images of these strangers had already become a part of my psyche.

By comparison, my closeup views of white people were cursory and fairly benign. I occasionally glimpsed their lives as I rode on the city bus along the main streets that linked our separate communities with the business and shopping district downtown. The contrasts were obvious. Their neighborhoods had big frame houses on side streets with canopies of oaks. Our neighborhoods had big frame houses divided into apartments on corners facing traffic. They had large lawns; we had small yards. Their skin was like flour with a little paprika mixed in it; ours was coffee with, or without, cream. But sometimes when I scanned them getting on or off the bus, I spotted something—the curve of a hip, the spread of a nose, the toss of a head, or sweep of an arm making a point—and I would swear for a moment, give or take several hours in the sun, I was watching some black person I knew.

The process of my acclimation was like the difference between watching black-and-white television and the movies. I started out with a limited, small-screen view of white people. We had obvious contrasts; some people played them up and could not relate to me, while others played them down and friendships formed. But the closer people get to each other, the more colors and shadings they see, the more they learn about each other, and the more details they pick up about the other—both the good and the bad. For instance, in my community I grew up hearing uttered at best as a backhand compliment, "Ah, hell. He's all right, I guess, for a 'cracker.'" But then I heard Florida southern whites drawl the word in a self-descriptive way and the sting of it was gone. Similarly, black people sling around the racial epithet "nigger" with each other like a sign of camaraderie, yet they're ready to fight if an outsider speaks the word. When I became a parent, I pronounced both words banned in our home.

I was taught much more subtle ways, subcategories, to distinguish the "others" even further. The white people who acted mean to us were probably the Klan or some kin, folks would say. Whites were jealous of us if we looked better or appeared better off than them. The older ones could not be trusted because they had hardened attitudes, and the younger ones might act all right for awhile, but just watch it—one day they would change. The good whites at best loaned us money sometimes, or at least they kept their distance and stayed out of our way. All the stories and warnings I heard permeated my life and gave a shape and form to the free-floating anxiety that surfaced while I was growing up. But as we all entered uncharted territory, our parents were probably the least prepared to equip us for the trip. Their experiences, their stories, differed from those we were creating. They urged us toward the future without realizing that something might be lost or left behind. Them.

Although I ate the good ol' southern cooking I was brought up on when Mama was around, in *my* kitchen jambalaya became my signature dish. I did stray in my youthful experimental times, however. My husband was game to try new concoctions, and I thrived on his enthusiasm.

Baked duck with orange sauce had to be kneaded first, then drained of fat as it slow-cooked. It took six hours for the Ghanian short ribs smeared with smooth peanut butter to fully cook. Curried chicken was served with several finger bowls of raisins, peanuts, coconut, and chutney as condiments. With most of these dishes I dreaded the work involved. My heart was never won over by them. A few years into our marriage, I noticed that when I prepared the other fancy dishes, my husband played the role of referee. He approved the menu, came into the kitchen from time to time to oversee the proceedings, then sat at the table and waited to be served. I watched him, waiting for the first sign of appreciation before I even touched anything on my plate. If what I had cooked was a hit, I got applause and a request to do it again. If I fouled out, I got a list of corrective measures to take next time. Either way, I lost my taste for the meal and only picked at my food.

But we equally enjoyed jambalaya, and both of us got involved in its preparation. We shopped for the meal together, conferring on the firmness of the peppers, the number of onions we wanted, whether we had a taste for more shrimp this time or could live with less ham. We negotiated on the amount of rice we needed to be sure we had enough for leftovers. Jambalaya was often served at our dinner parties, and a houseful of friends would stop by to savor it. They brought Greek salads, French desserts, German beer, and Italian wine. We provided the jazz and garlic bread. A few people begged to have the recipe, with varying degrees of success. Women who were older and purportedly wiser in their culinary ways tried it with their friends but invited me over first for a sample. Younger women sought a diagnosis when their experiments with meatless variations on the recipe failed.

Jambalaya requires patience. The disparate ingredients must be blended so that the flavors do not clash. The onions and garlic must be chopped, but not too fine, so that each piece can be tasted. The peppers should be sliced in thin long strips so that they wilt tenderly in the bacon's grease. The bacon must be cut into bite-sized pieces, then fried until the grease seeps out but before it gets crunchy. Canned whole tomatoes must first be drained and mashed. The ham can be purchased precooked, but it also has to be sliced in strips, and the shrimp must be carefully deveined. Chicken broth should be used instead of water, which makes the mixture too bland. And everything has to be ready, set, and waiting to be added at the precise moment when the grains of rice begin to gleam. I make jambalaya once in awhile now from memory, but after I sample a couple of spoonfuls, I give most of it away. For the next few days, I'm content just to sit and savor the pungent smell of thyme.

Recipe for Jambalaya

Ingredients

1 pound medium shrimp, cleaned and deveined
1 medium onion, diced
1 clove of garlic, chopped
1 green bell pepper, sliced into narrow strips
1 large can of tomatoes, drained and coarsely chopped
$1/4$ pound slice of boiled ham, cut into narrow, inch-long strips
$1/4$ pound bacon, cut into inch-long pieces
1 cup rice, raw
$1\,1/2$–2 cups chicken broth
Thyme
Salt and pepper

Directions

Use covered pan that goes from stove top to oven. Set oven to 350 degrees. Prepare all ingredients first. Heat pan on stove on medium-high setting. Fry bacon until it renders its fat but is not completely brown. Remove quickly, drain, and set aside. Add onion, bell pepper, and garlic and stir-fry until onion and garlic brown slightly and green pepper becomes limp. Add rice, stirring until milky. Then pour in tomatoes, ham, and $1\,1/2$ cups broth to start; add thyme and salt and pepper to taste, stirring continuously until ingredients begin to boil. Cover pan and place on rack in lower third of oven. Bake for 10–15 minutes, until rice begins to absorb liquid. Remove from oven and add shrimp, pressing pieces down into the bed of rice. Return to oven and bake for 15 minutes more. Add remaining broth if rice looks like it is drying out. Stir once. Serve with salad, warm bread, music, and friends.

SEEING BLACK AND WHITE AND COLORS

I was lost in the early evening stupor that usually descends upon me during one of my mother's visits from Jacksonville. For her, Florida's "Mason-Dixon line" cuts somewhere just below the greyhound dog track in Daytona Beach, and she crosses that line only a few times a year. The northern and southern parts of the state are separated by a cultural gulf as formidable as a mountain range. Traffic, crime, and political mayhem seem to increase with the trip south, but so does the action of big-city life. She expects to leave monotony for excitement when she travels here to Fort Lauderdale. So before she arrives, I spend weeks agonizing over how to come up with a schedule of activities to fill our days, but the choices have steadily dwindled. She still wistfully recalls memories from the 1970s, when we sat at ringside for a performance by country singer Barbara Mandrell, or shook hands backstage with the soul group The Dells, or watched a Broadway-bound play or an ice-skating revue.

I was working then as a feature writer and entertainment editor for the *Miami Herald* at a time when black reporters at a white newspaper were a rarity. Writing mostly human interest stories, where, regardless of color, people wanted to see me in order to get their moment of glory in the news, made the job easier in some ways. Still, over the years, there were often times when I was aware of holding my breath on a drive through a white neighborhood to a story, or in those first seconds when a new door opened and I walked into a room, never sure of what resistance I might find. A press pass and notebook are powerful weapons, however, capable of prying open lives. Once I was well inside, the revelations began. But after my work was finished, I sometimes dragged Mama along to the more glamorous encounters. For me these outings were an escape from the daily grind. We powdered, lipsticked, and perfumed ourselves and dressed in spangled earrings and Sunday clothes. I do not know if she realized how I clutched her elbow a little tighter as we made our way to the front of the room. But as I chattered on to keep her mind distracted, I was aware that her eyes stayed straight ahead, beyond the white audience, toward the stage.

Those days are long gone, however. In the 1980s I moved up to a twice-a-week observational newspaper column about women's issues and eclectic lifestyles in South Florida, subjects for which race did not matter—a rarity then for a black writer. I sent Mama copies of several of my articles written over the years, to show off my new status. I notice, however, that she has saved only the ones that mention her and the growing-up days in the old community. Anticipating her expectations when she comes to see me now, I guess I feel I must apologize for the relatively static pace of my life since the 1990s. I tape television programs instead of going out to see live theater; I prefer outdoor daytime concerts to nightclubs. Any extra stamina I muster is expended just keeping in phone, lunch, and dinner contact with old close friends. The writing I do now keeps me tied to a computer, mostly in solitude, instead of scouring press releases, mingling at cocktail parties, and handing out business cards on the prowl for the next day's potential front-page human interest story. So once Mama arrives, the best I can usually come up with is a movie or a buffet dinner; otherwise, the regimen is shopping and cooking each day. Then come the twilight hours, when we wait for the grandchildren to fit us into their busy adult lives. Often the wait lasts late into the night. By the time the network television news goes off, we are getting sleepy or rambling on in a verbal free-for-all.

This particular night, one of her questions stung me wide awake. "Don't

At the *Miami Herald* circa 1981.

you have any *black* friends?" It had come in the non sequitur way we have of jumping from subject to subject with interruptive ease—from sex to relationships to God to aches and pains—finishing each other's sentences or cutting them off. But this question paused and dangled between us. As she lay on the futon and I sat on the rattan chair a few feet away, a picture window of sunset seemed the only safe spot for us both to stare. The subject was territory we usually avoided, despite the fact that a certain degree of candor had crept into our conversations as we advanced in years. But this topic was difficult. Defenses raised, I rattled off a few names that I thought would satisfy her, even conjuring up some people I rarely see. As quickly as the question had stabbed the air, her attention bounced over to something else, and I was released—for the moment. But I knew I would never have an answer to appease her. She does not understand how my life ended up like this, given the way I was raised. And when I am forced to think about it, neither do I. Since college in the 1960s, a parade of people have marched in and out of my life with such frequency that I remember only a quarter of their names. A face pops up in my mind with a pleasant or disturbing memory, then flits by to make room for the next person I encounter. As for the ones I do recall, she has met, heard about, or glimpsed enough of them in photos to know they do not look like her or me.

To make it even more interesting, the question had come after a busy day that included lunch with one of my sister-friends. The woman, a decade younger than I, had served a deli spread, entertaining us like family in a home that is a decorator's delight. Antiques and art deco, overstuffed sofas and china, and rooms as inviting as the golf course view. We laughed through most of the meal at silly things I cannot even remember, trading recipes and enjoying each other's company. I can still see my friend's mischievous green eyes and hear her warm-hearted southern drawl. I have known her for years, but still I know I am this woman's only real black friend. We talk about it sometimes. She speculates that in her life she encounters so few black women, and those she does meet do not show much interest in developing a relationship. She wonders why; I have an idea. The gulf between black and white is just too wide for many people to try to cross on their own, without prompting. Some fear they will drown in the pain and confusion, so they avoid it. Others try, but find rough waters and struggle because they cannot stay afloat. And those who do jump in and get far enough away from their shore can find themselves getting caught up in crosscurrents, too.

I have had whites tell me, "Gee, I don't think of you as being black" and think it is a compliment. Sometimes I just nod and, relieved, they change the subject. The astute ones may spot the perplexed look on my face and stammer, "What I meant was . . . you don't *act* like a black person. I mean, most black people are hard to get to know. . . . You know what I mean." Sometimes I say what I really feel: "But if you don't think of me as being black, that means that you have to erase my color in order to deal with me as a human being." Then they get defensive and accuse me of being overly sensitive or militant. To me, they are saying my color is a negative, a barrier to their friendship. They cannot deal with my blackness *and* deal with me as a person at the same time. The remark may be made in an earnest attempt to prove they have transcended thinking about race to relate on a human level. Instead, what it shows me is the power of negative racial images to affect relationships, even with people who have good intentions.

The initial hint of the wider implications of this phenomenon came during one of my first jobs in college at the Foreign Student Center, where I got a double dose of culture shock. It was my responsibility to read the letters of application that came across my desk and send form-letter responses. I loved the postmarks in magentas, greens, and purples instead of just red, white, and blue, and as the return addresses of cities in Africa, Asia, Australia, and Europe filed in each day, I felt as if I were taking armchair trips around the world. The potential students wrote in neat pen and awkward English about how they loved America and its freedom and how much an education here would mean. They were welcomed at first, only to get caught up in America's puzzling racial complex. The Africans and East Indians, in particular, came into the office indignantly protesting the discrimination they encountered, based on the color of their skin, when they tried to rent apartments or eat at restaurants. They ended up isolating themselves from Americans, especially blacks, and associating only with other internationals to protect themselves, their psyches. The roots of my curiosity about multicultural issues must have been planted then.

I, too, have moved to another culture, and I have learned how to adapt to the language and customs of the hosts fairly well. I have spent the majority of my life in the company of white people. In most social settings I am still either one of only a few blacks present or the only one. A black friend of mine suggests that this is because I have traveled for so long in such "a rarefied atmosphere" as a journalist who works with people from the majority culture. But what about those people, black and white, who were born and raised in racially mixed surroundings and yet choose to live separate, antagonistic lives? Environment cannot be the only deciding factor. Some of us have been shoved into the racial gulf by a series of strange circumstances, and our view of people *had* to change, like making the shift from seeing only black and white to seeing colors.

When I was a young girl and Mama arrived home from work exhausted, she hurriedly shimmied out of her white uniform with the onion smell and the meat splatters and left it behind her on the floor like shed skin. For a few years, she wore one like it to cook and serve hot lunches to students at a white elementary school across town, a job that promised security. But she had to leave home—and me—before sunrise to get to work, and something had to give, so it was the job. Now she worked ten hours a day in a hotel kitchen, mixing salads and decorating sandwich trays. "I make the best tuna and egg salad, and my relish trays are beautiful, if I must say so myself," she boasted to her friends. But at night she brought her frustration home to me. "I don't want you to ever have to work as hard as I've had to work," she said wearily one of those evenings as she slipped into her house dress and headed for the kitchen. "I could have been a practical nurse by now," she grumbled, almost to herself. I had heard the story before about how her parents refused to pay for her schooling. "But why didn't you just go on your own?" I asked. I expected her to launch into some story about wanting so much to have me, but she attacked. "I didn't have the opportunities you're going to have," she snapped. Her irritation stung me, as if I had somehow taken something of hers away.

Mama popped open a tall Schlitz and went on the porch to unwind and left me wondering. What opportunities? The jobs in black stores and offices were sought after; they went fast, and somebody's relatives always got places near the front of the line. A couple of my teachers in high school talked as if it were understood that with a college education many of us would go into their field. The work was respectable and secure. The only question was the subject—shop, gym, music, social studies, English, or a foreign language, in that ascending order. I made no connection that the future might involve a new group of "other" people, because the possibilities seemed limited, at best, or demeaning, from what I could see.

I remember Mama wearing a white uniform only one time when some kind of food service was not involved. It was one of those "real down times," as she called it. I also remember the way she acted when she came home that day. A strange blue car dropped her off, and I forgot about asking her who it was when I saw the two large paper bags she was lugging up in the stairs in either arm. "Never again!" she said as she threw both of them down on the floor and stalked off to the bedroom to undress. I dug into the bags with both hands, pulling out clothes—a long, wrinkled dress, a blouse with buttons missing, a scarf with curious painted faces. Disappointed, I looked deeper but still saw nothing I could wear. "Don't even bother," she called out from the other room. "That's just some crap this woman passed off on me 'cause she was only paying me ten dollars for cleaning her house." Later, she dumped the bags in the garbage can. "I'll do a lot of things, but I'm not going to scrub nobody's nasty toilet again but mine," she said with disgust. "And you, either." A couple of years later, I cleaned toilets and floors and dishes for a short time for five dollars a week, but I was cleaning the home of a *black* woman, a teacher, which made all the difference.

Now, as I retraced Mama's steps, I picked up the trail she left, sorting the underwear and support hose into one stack for handwashing and the uniform into a much larger pile that we later dropped off at the laundry she used to do our heavy clothes every week. The newspapers and television ran advertisements for automatic washing machines, and a few people we knew had the old wringer models, but we still scrubbed small items on a washboard in the bathtub and hung them out to dry on a backyard clothesline. Instead of a self-defrosting refrigerator-freezer, we had to work like arctic explorers with an ice pick just to extract chunks of ice to make a cold drink. These days, I forget to use my icemaker and I buy paper plates to avoid the dishwasher. My clothes are chosen because they are wrinkle-free and go to the neighborhood dry cleaners. I do not even own an ironing board. But, still, I had known early on that I wanted some of the luxuries. Opportunity came one winter afternoon in my senior year.

The quiet was welcome as I sat in my high school English class that day. While the other students pondered some William Wordsworth stanzas, I struggled with an essay for an oratorical contest. Mrs. Curry, the teacher, had spotted the announcement and urged me to enter. The speech was to be fifteen minutes on some weighty topic like "The Challenge of the Youth of America Today" delivered from memory for a first prize of

$150 in cash. From time to time she glanced over at me above her glasses, the wrinkles smoothing in her stern beige face as she gave me the quick encouraging smile that showed her favoritism. My hunched shoulders relaxed a little. As it was, the two colleges to which I had applied in Washington, D.C., and North Carolina had accepted me, just as the recruiters had predicted, but then we figured the costs. "Baby, this is more than I make in a year," Mama said, pushing the papers aside and breaking my heart as she closed two doors. My choices now seemed to lie with the three in-state black colleges, but spring was approaching and it was already too late to apply. I gnawed on the eraser and wrote more words without meaning, dreading what my future would be. I had even more dread of the reactions from the Miss-Its when I had to admit that I had dreamed too big.

The box above the blackboard came alive like rustling cellophane, and tapping on the microphone signaled that an announcement was coming. "Will the following students report . . ." it began, and I hardly realized that I was holding my breath, braced for trouble, until the gasp of air escaped when my name was called. Mrs. Curry was the first to come over and pat me on the shoulder with congratulations. I was one of thirteen in a class of over four hundred to score high enough on the required statewide exam to warrant admission into one of the newly integrated white state universities. I tried to shrug it off at first. I did not even know the name of one of these universities, I said. And besides, they sounded too close to home for me. But what the heck. I would attend the luncheon the principal was inviting us to that afternoon. Who knew what a difference a meal could make?

We gathered in one of the classrooms for boxes of Kentucky Fried Chicken. As we started to eat, a young white man unwrapped himself from a chair and appeared in front of us. He had legs that went on forever, and his gaze of hazy marble eyes seemed to lock onto mine while he talked, as if pleading for understanding. I held a napkin in front of my mouth to hide the grease and tried to pick daintily at my food. The young man, whose name was Dan, was a graduate student at the University of Florida, he said, and president of the Freedom Party, an off-campus protest group self-designated to recruit black freshmen because the university would not. He had driven north from Gainesville, a small Central Florida town of cows and self-proclaimed rednecks, to invite us to travel to the campus and visit for a day, at our own expense. Other blacks were there, he promised, some transfer students, though admittedly not many. Still, some of the admission fees could be waived to pave our way if we decided to enter. The trip involved two hours each way on a school day, he said. My ears perked up with more than casual interest then. Two hours. That would be the farthest I had ever traveled on my own. How difficult the struggle must have been for Mama, hovering between pride at her secondhand achievement and fear of the alien environment I wanted to enter. But she said yes and scraped together the money for the Greyhound bus ticket that she must have known would eventually take me away from her for good.

Five of us traveled there that day from my high school, loosely acquainted and linked only by our curiosity. The tour, my first look at a college campus, went by in a blur of impressions: bustling, strange, wide open, complex. We were told that money was available through a new War on Poverty Program just signed into law by President Johnson offering a package of grants, loans, and work-study to the poor but proud. That was us. The problem was Mama. Would she agree? For a lunch break during the visit, we gathered in a restaurant across from campus and ate at separate tables with different hosts, based on our interests: pre-med, psychology, economics. I sat at the "undecided" table and absorbed. In those surroundings, in the company of so many white people, I felt odd but not uncomfortable; instead of a tight shoe, I had some breathing room. Then I spotted a dark-skinned flash of blue blazer and gold buttons filing in with a group of others in the mostly white Freedom Party. I watched him at another table, trading jokes with such ease and confidence. Fitting in. As his spurts of laughter sprinkled the room, arms animated, I got a fleeting look at his spidery fingers, long and graceful in the expansive gesture. I knew that was the way I wanted to be—in that place with those people and with someone like him.

That evening, I waited for Mama to come home. The television droned on, but every time I tried to concentrate, nervous excitement stirred me again. I had to play this right. Wait until she got in and changed clothes. Maybe I should have a beer open and waiting for her. No. Too obvious. Once she was comfortable on the couch, I started. "I need to talk to you about something," I said in my most serious voice. Too much. She looked startled. I plunged ahead anyway. "UF looked really good, and I think I can get in and money's available, too, they said." Did I cover all the bases? The prospect that I would go to college had loomed for awhile, out there somewhere in the future. Now it was within a few months' reach. I could see the weight of that realization cloud Mama's face. It read, *You mean you'd want to leave me?* She looked incredulous. Well, no, I could not say *that*. But I wanted to go to college. She got up and went into the kitchen to fix herself something to eat. "I've been thinking about it," she said later. Good sign. I was afraid when she had said nothing. "If my folks had let me go to a nursing school out of town like I wanted, my life would have turned out so much better," she said. Her voice sounded as though it were coming to me from far away, but that was a *yes*. I did not want to get too happy yet. I told her about the financial aid papers she would have to fill out, the ones that stated exactly how much—or how little—she made. And we would need help to do it. The thoughtful silence was nearly as long this time. She came back with an idea—one of our neighbors was a single mother with a daughter in a black women's college. She was "pretty regular," Mama said. We would ask her. As we sat at that woman's dining room table and Mama shyly spilled out the true financial particulars of our lives for the first time on paper, protectiveness swelled up in me. I saw what a miracle she had created the past seventeen years in her own resourceful Geechee way.

The letter of acceptance arrived within a month after I submitted my application. I carried the paper to school with me, unfolding it from my purse like a banner to show to the incredulous students and counselors. The trembling inside started around then, along with a feeling of being empty and drained. The struggle had ended—I was getting out—but an undercurrent of fear remained. Would I know how to act, or would I make a fool of myself? What would they expect of me? What if I failed? But some changes can come so quickly and be so transforming that it is impossible to prepare for them.

For the rest of my senior year I lived on two planes of existence: one immersed in graduation activities and the other rehearsing my essay for the oratorical contest with my English teacher, Mrs. Curry. In a way, the repetitive drills of memory recall and rote recitation became the one piece of reality I could grasp as the world I knew grew more unfocused and slowly dissolved. Mama had to work, so Mrs. Curry drove me to the contest in another black part of town. As my teacher walked me to the backstage of the high school auditorium, she put her hand on my shoulder. "You know what you have to do. Now do it," she said in her no-nonsense kind of way. She was one of those light-skinned, wavy-haired bourgeois women of her generation who taught practical grammar skills and had gone into teaching to uplift the race. But she nudged me into literature. *You will be a teacher someday,* she correctly predicted. Wishing me good luck, she disappeared to take a seat out front.

Five of us finalists, all female, sat in folding chairs lined up against a wall behind the stage. All I could see was the back of a black curtain and steps leading to it. One by one, they called each of us up to deliver our fifteen-minute speech by heart, without notes. One rambled on in a monotone and ended to polite applause that put her out of the running. The next two sounded stronger, but I was fourth and concentrating on my opening. My name was called, and for a moment, the first words drained from my head as the blood pulsed through my legs, rushing me forward and up and over to the lectern. I was vaguely aware of people shifting in their chairs behind me, but the spotlight was on. The words spilled out like building blocks and bounced around the quiet room. I knew exactly where they were headed and how to guide each phrase in the right direction. Until the end. A few of my final words stumbled through my lips, but I finished quickly and hurried back to my seat, kicking myself yet glad that at least I had done it. I barely listened as the fifth contestant stammered through.

Shortly, after all five speeches had been completed, the treasurer of the black women's organization called the names, starting with third place. After the second place announcement, my hopes sagged a little. It was down to three of us, all hoping for first place. A sympathy vote for the stammerer? I wondered. When she and the monotone speaker turned toward me and clapped, I realized my name was being called again. I did not believe it. But my name was right there on the certificate that I showed Mrs. Curry on our way home in her car. First prize, $150—enough to sustain me for a term at the college of my choice. And that decision, which would set me adrift in the gulf, had already been made.

On a visit back home during a break between terms, Mama sat beside me at the kitchen table and started filling me in on the happenings since I had been gone. A man who used to go to our church was working as a mail carrier now, she said. "He was always one of those folks who had gumption, though, and you need that with white folks or they'll walk all over you. I know them. Worked around them all my life." Someone I did not know had gotten on the police force, and Mama insisted I must remember him. "He graduated ahead of you." But I could not conjure up a face. It was a big deal all right, in a town known for its bigotry. But before I could say that, she chimed in. "He's having a hard time. 'They' don't really *want* us around. 'They' smile in your face and pretend, but they'll stab you in the back on GP [general principle] if you don't look out." The phone company was taking applications, she said, but it's only because they *have* to hire a few black operators. So if I applied there for a summer job, I'd better not expect to get a call back. In fact, why even bother to go? "Ok," I decided, "I'll just work on campus all summer," glancing over at her for a reaction. But she just shrugged. I could not believe how much the talk around town now centered so much on "them."

The Strand's neon marquee still offered black-and-white and technicolor refuge for me, but the seats creaked and felt unsteady, as though the bolts were loosening from the floor. If I thought that was bad, folks said, roaches and rats had invaded the other two theaters, thanks to all those greasy french fries they allowed. Some of my young cousins in junior high were in the first experiment with integrated schools, and the one who showed off his report card full of A's in elementary school was now cutting school to hang out with older kids on "the blocks." Those streets still teemed with people, color, music, and banners hawking prices that did not just look like bargains—they looked dirt cheap. In a window or two, you would see a "For Sale or Lease" sign. The undercurrent of discomfort that was injected into our lives while I was in high school was growing stronger, or perhaps just more noticeable.

At college, intraracial alliances also began to shift. In our own segregated communities we had a social barometer to establish our distinctions. Now we were all being lumped together, despite differences as indelible as the tribal markings of our African ancestors when they were forcibly grouped as slaves. My roommate and I had obviously been paired by race with the assumption that we had a natural affinity. We did bond quickly, but we had little in common otherwise, and by the end of the year we were barely speaking to each other. The next year, the dorm advisors tried a different approach and assigned incoming freshmen by background and presumed affinities. A black girl from the elite crowd in my hometown whom I knew only by reputation had enrolled. Her parents owned a big business, and she was "New-York-City-for-the-holidays" bourgeoisie and out of my league. The white freshman from Palm Beach who was supposed to be the girl's roommate took one look at her, stamped her foot, and demanded another room. The upper-crust black girl sought comfort by spending time in my room instead of alone in her own, and within the year she was gone. There have always been all kinds of black people, and now some new ones like me were being spawned.

I tried to hold onto some of the old ways—really I did. I had illusions for awhile that music might move me into the mainstream, as it had with some others I had read about. Motown, the Detroit phenomenon that eventually went uptown to Los Angeles, was the mecca of opportunity for young black entertainers at that time—the late 1960s and early 1970s. But after working awhile and starving awhile, I just did not have the staying power. So I drifted off in a direction of my own, as one who reports instead of one who performs.

One weeknight, as the baby-sitter waited in the living room entertaining our two children, my husband and I put on the final touches of our evening wear for another one of those nights out as an entertainment writer. We were headed for the opening of a big-name act at a local hotel at the height of the winter nightclub season. New hairdo. Nice jewelry. Formal wear. We glided out of the house and to the car on looks of appreciation from the household and still felt the glow as we strolled into the ballroom together. Halfway down the layer cake of terraces and stairs, I caught a snatch of murmuring from a white-haired head below eye level. Folds of iridescent purple smoothed out across my stomach as I inhaled, bracing for the compliment. "I wonder how much *that* costs." The voice seemed to boom up at me like an off-kilter blow. He assumed I was a woman for hire. I know I was not the only one who heard. Because I could not see him, and I did not want to, I just kept on walking, holding a bitter breath until I sat down and pulled out my pen and paper to do my job. That memory remains so strong, even after all these years. Sometimes I try to diminish its effect by wisecracking that there is an endless supply of white people for me to draw on—or discard. Sometimes I just bloom where I am planted, even in polluted soil. In truth, I have learned best to submerge my feelings and reactions in order to survive. Discouragement still seems to lurk beneath the surface of black-white relations for my generation. Our children's generation, on the other hand, seems to be better at crossing the color boundaries. They were born to do it; others of us must learn—and relearn—as we go along.

I was thinking about that the other morning when I made a call to a potential swimming instructor. It was as difficult as I thought, conceding failure and trying to make things right. Third time, you are out. Or, maybe, third time is a charm. Shuttled from one voice to another, I had to tell my story again each time, explaining that I am determined to start lessons again after two abortive attempts and that I am determined to learn to swim in this lifetime. I had managed to fake my way through some touchy situations, starting in college. We were supposed to pass a mandatory swimming test as freshmen, but I had never set foot in a pool. After whining and tears wore down the instructor, I bargained my way into the same teacher's folk-dancing class and traveling troupe simply by getting wet in the pool and climbing out again. I clogged my way through Polish, Greek, and Yiddish melodies, caught up so much in the intricate movements that I sometimes forgot how incongruous I must have looked beneath the kerchief, peasant blouse, and dirndl skirt. A vague dissatisfaction lingered despite the bargain. One day, I said, I would learn. And I tried. Five one-hour sessions once. Three sessions another. Each time something came up before I made it to the end of the series of classes.

As I told the teacher during this phone call, I can ease myself down the stairs into the pool and bob my head in and out again quickly to get acclimated. Once my courage is up, I can stretch out, hands shoulder level and steady, and feel the lift of my feet propel me like a cotton ball in the wind as I kick ever so lightly, eyes open and straight ahead, eager to see. Then, short of air, I try to reach up for a breath but end up swallowing water, and I panic as I flail back to the safe edge. The times when I attempted to just float on a raft, encouraged by friends, my bottom half sank and weighed me down. What worked for them did nothing for me. I thought it was important for me to set a good example for my kids by taking classes and dispelling my fear of the water, but they have outshone me, doing it their way. My daughter was diving into the deep end by first grade and waterskiing during summers at camp. My son hated the regimen of lessons as a toddler but learned through trial and error with older friends how to do well enough to save himself and enjoy the experience.

As entertainment writer, with singer Billy Davis at Diplomat Hotel opening.

Still, both of them rarely even think about swimming—they can take it or leave it. I, on the other hand, am the one who muses about it all the time.

Maybe that is because, unlike them, my mother could not afford lessons for me at the neighborhood recreation pool. So when I used to visit, I spent most of my time reading the bulletin boards where civil rights activities were listed. They seemed safer to me. But sometimes I stood at a distance watching the other kids doing belly flops and playing as if they were in a sandlot instead of a potential watery grave. That was how I saw it—a view inherited from Mama, who even closes her eyes when she rides across a steep bridge over the St. John's River. But she did sail on her first cruise ship at seventy, reminding me that there is hope, that things can always change.

After Mama leaves, my green-eyed friend has urged me to bring a bathing suit over and leave it at her home. She has new hello-hugging, house-key-sharing, coffee-drinking neighbors she wants me to meet—a black retired couple. Every now and then she calls Mama long distance just to say hello, and Mama looks forward to their conversations now. I can practice in my friend's pool with privacy as I learn how to keep my head up and breathe.

COUSINS

*T*he meeting was in one of those wide, boxy condominium recreation halls where neighbors gather to quibble over bridge games or debate the merits of painting walls sand-colored or beige. But the hosts for this party had brightened up the place by tying symbolic clusters of black, white, yellow, and red balloons to some of the folding chairs circling the room. Middle Eastern women with waist-length ebony hair and short silk dresses comforted children falling asleep in their fathers' arms. West Indian voices lilted, and laughter bubbled thick and saucy from two large brown-skinned women huddled near the door. A slender dark man with an African kinte cloth scarf around his jacket came up and introduced himself as "chief," then just bobbed his head up and down in a series of polite nods and smiles, body language substituting for a lack of words. A stately black woman with graying hair wearing a pantsuit of African print introduced herself as Sarah Goldstein—"Yes, Jewish; fools everybody," she said—and I tried not to looked surprised. She clasped my hands warmly and steered me into the room with others gathered for the meeting on multicultural understanding.

I was there to learn some techniques for conducting workshops to help people learn to accept racial and ethnic differences. This was a new role for me. As a journalist, I wrote about immigrants who had begun to flock to Florida, transforming the cultural complexion of what was once a "good ol' boy" southern state. Then for some reason people started calling me, thinking I had something to say. A colleague in the diversity business had shared research with me over the years as I struggled to absorb as much as I could about human social patterns, cramming for an exam that would never be over. She had invited me to this event. I scanned the room once more, sure now that she would not be coming, and fought off the urge to turn around and head back out the door. But the name of the group, the Institute for the Healing of Racism, was intriguing. A couple of dozen chapters have sprung up around the country since the mid-1980s, and the mission of this new branch in South Florida was to conduct workshops where people could talk openly about racial and ethnic problems and seek solutions. This party was a first step, an open house, a way of bringing people together for some one-on-one encounters.

As the room filled, I edged into a corner to watch. People drifted toward me from the soft-drink bar to the food table, stopping to greet one another with a hug, a handshake, eye contact—some acknowledgment. After awhile, in the blur of humanity, the different-colored faces lost all their distinctiveness. "This is great, isn't it?" I had not been aware of the white man standing next to me sampling the macadamia nut pie. He was short and balding with an egg-shaped midsection that gave his stomach a sharp curve at the belt buckle. His tie hung crookedly over his tightly stretched shirt. Looking at him brought to my mind an unpleasant experience from my past and made me feel a familiar twinge of suspicion. Instant dislike. I saw shadiness and malice beneath his benign navy blue suit. He looked just like the North Florida salesman at Sears who had laughed in my face that summer day in 1964 when, newly empowered by the approaching implementation of the Civil Rights Act, I got the shaky courage to stop in his department and ask him for a job. My embarrassment when he told me I could not work there because I was black was not enough for him. He called out to me as I was leaving, his voice dripping with salaciousness: "Tell you what, honey. You can clean my house anytime." He wanted my humiliation.

The white man at the table now stood with his beefy hand outstretched.

Multicultural gathering for video diversity project.

"My name is Don." He was one of the people involved in getting the institute started locally, he explained. I shook his hand and introduced myself. "What this is all about is cleaning out all the garbage that's in here," he said as he thumped his ample chest. "It's deep in here—in the heart. And it's ugly. You've got to wrench it out." His earnest eyes locked on mine. I relaxed and listened as his conversation took a peculiar turn. "I'm from Illinois. And I just wasn't aware. I didn't experience it until I went in the army," he said. "Raleigh, North Carolina. I went into this restaurant and sat down, and this black woman came up and she curled her lips and said, 'You can't sit here.' I said, 'Why not?' and I was told it was for blacks only. That's when I first saw the separate water fountains and all." He shook his head sadly. The "it" word of racism hung there for a moment, a shadow lurking in the corner of a well-lit room. Born and raised a thousand miles apart, we had each learned about "it"; we had been brought up well. The pendulum of emotion "it" stirred up—swallowed rage or resignation—had cut deeply into both of us in some way.

Sarah Goldstein made the announcement for everyone to be seated because the program was about to start. Don took my plate and dumped it out along with his. We said goodbye and headed toward seats in different parts of the room. A young, white, bearded guitarist accompanied an older black singer with a jazzy Al Jarreau style. They sang songs about

With diversity video co-producer Barrie Brett.

world peace and racial harmony. Two women from St. Louis spoke—inspirational, poetic: one white, the other black. "We're all related," one of them said early on. Familiar, like family. "We're fifty-second cousins to everyone we meet." Intellectually, I understood the women's concept, and I advocate it in my workshops. But the explanation seemed too simple for such a complex issue. Besides, when something is triggered "deep in here—in the heart," as Don put it, we do not operate by intellect. Whether or not we like to admit it, race colors our perceptions about other people, regardless of what race is doing the judging. Maybe some baseline genetic racial programming exists, programming that makes us instinctively dislike those who look different from us. Just human nature, people say. Simple answer again.

The women kept talking and I tried to pay attention, but I found myself mentally leafing through the pages of material in a file back home. Sharper minds than mine—psychologists, anthropologists, geneticists, philosophers—are still wrestling with this question from different angles, and they cannot seem to come to a consensus, either, even though they have gone pretty far back to start looking at why we behave the way we do. It took millions of years and several variations for the first humans to evolve into *Homo sapiens*—modern man, according to archaeologists' findings. About one hundred thousand years ago, *Homo sapiens* took a giant evolutionary step forward. They learned how to walk and talk and make things with their hands, and they set off wandering. Over the next forty thousand years or so, they spread out around the globe. For all that activity, however, when it comes to civilized behavior among ourselves, we are novices. We have only been at it about ten thousand years. So no wonder we are still fighting this out. Researchers have reported discovery of a common gene in all humans, and they have even pared it down to the same grandmother generations ago, a specimen nicknamed Lucy. Still, this idea of interrelationship is controversial. The idea of different races is more popular, because it can be used to explain the obvious physical differences caused by our migrations around the globe. But in fact what we call "race" today is a concept that has only emerged fairly recently in evolutionary history, the last twenty thousand years or so—just ten thousand years longer than we have tried to be civilized. And here we are, thousands of years later, still trying to unlearn some uncivilized behavior toward each other because of our differences. One psychologist claimed, at a seminar I once attended, that the genetic changes that had occurred were very superficial, that the whole concept of "race" was created for political reasons. If human beings were racially different, he pointed out, they would not be able to reproduce, or if they did some aberration would result, as when the mating of a donkey and horse produces an infertile mule.

We may see ourselves in terms of colors or "subspecies"—black, white, yellow, red—created by the environments where our ancestors happened to live, but we were also meant to be mobile and to migrate and mix and blend. Still, we often fight the inevitable. Deep down we know we are alike, and yet we feel we are different. Our human behavior defies logic. Given the option of mixing or staying separate, most people tend to associate with people who look like them, and as a society we encourage that. Just human nature, we say. If some insist that they are drawn together not because of skin color but because of the way they look at the world and their role in it, others argue that that concept should have *everything* to do with race. Circular, certainly. But if, as the woman said, we are all relatives—cousins fifty-two times removed—we humans are just a dysfunctional family, playing favorites and nursing grudges like wounded children. And whenever we try to get together, we should expect some bittersweet moments, but there is no way of ridding ourselves of one another. Now that made some sense to me.

I was raised by my mother and her relatives, and what they told me about the other side of the family had subtly shaped my perceptions. I learned early which of my people I was to favor. The "others" were small-town rural Florida people—more clannish, I heard—and I surmised that it was uncomfortable to be around them. During the rare encounters I had with my father's branch of the family, experience confirmed my preconceived attitudes. I eventually learned more, bit by bit. My paternal grandmother was a pale, stout, reticent woman. Her father was a slave, freed at the age of thirteen. He became a traveling minister and married a bright young schoolteacher, a mulatto who gave her daughters light skin and black, wavy hair. My grandmother fell in love with a tenant farmer, and after my father was born in the hard financial times of the 1930s, she moved with him from Georgia to farmland in Central Florida. The few times I remember visiting, she baked, stewed, and boiled fresh country food, trying her best to appease me, and I grumbled because there were gnats outside and no television. She kept a wad of snuff tucked inside her bottom lip and smelled like stale cigarette smoke when I kissed her hello. The first time I had to go to the bathroom at her house, I was directed through the yard to an outhouse. When I finished, I made the mistake of turning around to look in the hole. From a layer of deepest darkness, maggots swarmed up to the rim as furious as my fear of these strange people, their customs, and their ways. The stench turned my stomach and I gagged. For the rest of the weekend, I ran into the woods and crouched behind a tree when I had to go. My fear of grass snakes was not nearly as great as my disgust at facing that rancid, interminable abyss.

That seems to be the way it is with us human beings. We may be biologically related, but if separated in some way, like placing us in different countries and darkening or lightening our skin with genetics, we start claiming to be better than others. Then we interpret everything that happens to us in such a way that we reinforce our mistaken belief. As the women speaking at the antiracism seminar put it, sometimes we just have to go deep to find common ground; and we know how perplexing family can be anyway.

I married and had two children; my father died in the late 1970s, when they were barely school-aged, without ever seeing them. I had had no contact with his sisters and brothers or their children after his demise. Then one day several years later, my mother called me and said she had received a letter. "It's from your aunt," my mother said. "They're planning a family reunion and they want you to come and bring the kids." The reunion was being held just a few miles from my home on a weekend when I did not have to work. Still, I hesitated. Would I feel comfortable if I went? Intellectually I understood that we had a genetic tie, but emotionally I felt as disconnected from them as I would feel among strangers with whom I was forced to associate. Among my mother's relatives, on the other hand, we visited each other—not often, but enough to establish a rapport. There were seven cousins of my generation in her family, and I had a couple of favorites. I had played the big sister role to one of the girls, combing her hair, taking her to movies, and sharing snacks and secrets when she spent the night with my mother and me. The other cousin I had watched grow from a shy, awkward adolescent into a cocky young man who enjoyed nightclubs and spirited conversations as much as I did. We spent time together, getting to know and understand each other. But this "other family" was unfamiliar to me.

My father's youngest sister had arranged our first meeting at a restaurant over breakfast, hoping that the camaraderie of a meal would ease the estrangement. We talked about the antics of my children, whom they would meet later. My aunt's oldest daughter sat next to her, across from me, and I could feel her eyes peering at me as I babbled on, feeling increasingly nervous at her microscopic attention. We paid our bill at the cash register and walked out to the parking lot together. The cousin walked behind, and I slowed my pace to hers. I began asking her questions. She was a computer operator and took courses at a business college, she explained. At eighteen, after high school graduation, she had a child by choice, and she was raising her six-year-old daughter alone in a house she owned. "I admire that. Raising a family is something I could never have done alone. That's why I got married so young," I said, surprising even myself with the admission. Talk flowed slowly but a little more easily. By the time we reached my car, the expression on her face had shifted out of neutral. "You know something?" she asked. I paused with my key in the car door. "I've always heard that you were stuck-up. Thought you were better than us," she said. Perceptions, working both ways.

At the reunion picnic later that day, my children scampered around the park with *their* generation of newfound cousins. My daughter, thirteen at the time, was the special one to watch. We had adopted her when she was five weeks old. She was a biracial baby, the product of an interracial relationship in the early 1970s that did not have a chance socially, but in this expanding black family she found the security of identity. At one point she rushed over, tugging the hand of another vaguely familiar girl about her age behind her like she was holding found money. They had been neighborhood playmates when they were younger and my daughter beamed, "She's in our family." The two had not been friendly since they entered adolescence, and they did not become buddy-buddy again after that meeting; they just enjoyed acknowledging the family connection. This branch of my family had rarely been discussed at home, so my children did not meet them with the same preconceived notions I had. "Children may have their preferences," a psychologist once told me, "but they only show prejudice when they are actively taught negative things about others by people in their own group. That means prejudice is not a natural instinct, it's all learned," she said.

I sought out that same cousin later in the evening because at least she was familiar. We sat at the same table, listening to music, and tried to make conversation. "You know, I've been looking around all day, and I haven't seen a single person who looks like me," I said. I inherited my mother's legs and my father's eyes, but not much of their facial features. "Maybe Aunt Virginia, Mama's aunt. I remember her when I was little. She was pretty," the cousin said. I looked around expectantly. "Her boyfriend killed her when she was young," she added. I gave up on my search for familiarity. Leaning back in the chair with a sigh, I kicked off one of my high heels, a common habit, careful to keep them out of full view because of embarrassment, not propriety. I flexed my relieved foot and massaged the toes. "I do that a lot," she said, watching me curiously. "No kidding?" "Yeah. I've got this big knot below my big toe that hurts like hell sometimes," she said, taking off her flats. There we were, sitting off to ourselves in the corner of a room at a gathering of family, comparing our feet. And sure enough, we just had to look for it—look really deep, to find the painful parts, to find the common bond.

ZORAVILLE

*T*he last few stragglers jostled me awake, lugging their pillows and suitcases, avoiding eye contact as if doing penance for causing the half-hour delay. I shifted shoulders and checked the lighted dial on the watch of the woman sitting across from me. 5:30 A.M. We were losing time just standing still. Once they all found seats, the charter bus groaned and belched smoke as it pulled onto the highway out of Fort Lauderdale for the four-hour ride. Just twenty black women, including me, on an overnight escape to Zoraville.

That is the name I have given the annual Zora Neale Hurston Festival in Eatonville, Florida. The tiny town just north of Orlando has two distinctions. It is the oldest surviving all-black municipality in the country, incorporated in 1887, and it is the hometown of Hurston—an anthropologist and controversial writer of the Harlem Renaissance—whose career peaked in the 1930s and 1940s and then took a sharp nosedive. She died in obscurity in 1960 at Fort Pierce, where she was buried only to be critically resurrected in the 1980s by feminist authors, most notably Alice Walker. As a result of the interest in her fiction and folklore of Florida's rural working poor, the state has given her honored-black-writer status. In January, her birth month, an arts celebration culminates with a weekend festival that gets national attention.

I had a reason for going, I told people, besides the fact that my students study her work at the university where I teach. She is a role model for me, not just in the literary sense. We are both Florida writers with strong black roots and white educations. She enjoyed researching and sampling other cultures, and so do I. And both of us like to tell stories; she got in trouble for doing it. I had heard that the country folks in Eatonville thought the Barnard graduate was too uppity, soaking up their lives, their language, their secrets, and telling them to the world. I had read how the black New York intellectuals berated her for acting too southern and "country" around white folks and adopting too many of their ways. The "Zora-telling" in her best-known novel, *Their Eyes Were Watching God,* is so compelling people swear it is autobiographical; and it is so obtuse in her autobiography, *Dust Tracks on a Road,* people swear she was lying about her life. I just love stories that are not easy to figure out.

As one of the many self-proclaimed daughters, black and white, who discovered the writer in the 1990s, I talked my way on board for this excursion to pay homage. A social club had organized the trip, but half the passengers, including me, were not members. We were working women, mothers, single, married, pre- and post-menopausal, using Zora as an escape from our regular lives. We all came with baggage, but we packed lightly, as if we expected to return with more than we had when we left home. As we began to rouse at daybreak, the club member who invited me made some introductions. I dismissed the initial uneasiness I felt as the shyness that usually surfaces when I am around strangers without a notebook, without a shield. Having made her way to where I was sitting, I heard her say, "—and this is my writer-friend." The women nodded with the fake smile you give a salesman who knocks at your door. They clutched their belongings a little tighter and quickly shifted their gaze.

I curled up and stretched my legs across two empty seats, out of sight, beyond scrutiny. The uneasy feeling subsided on the waves of conversation. "Take that!" A chorus of disappointed sighs swelled from the whist game in the back of the bus. "Honey, I'm hot now. Watch my heat." "You better fan yourself with these." Cards slapped down on the table to a new, even more vocal round of discontent. "Stop this bus. Stop this damn bus right now!" The first player rose noisily, feigning insult. Startled heads swiveled to the back, eyes peered up and over the tops of seats. A disembodied voice rammed through the stillness. "You better check yourself before you be by yourself." After a flash flood of laughter, the game resumed quietly. "He just wanted to sit down on me after we got married. And he knew the kind of woman I was to begin with." The voice of the teacher sitting behind me rose up and curled itself around my ears as she talked to the woman next to her, an out-of-work secretary. "I thought he had something going for himself, too." "One of *those*, huh?" the secretary said. "I know what you mean. They *had* a job, a car, everything— before they met you. And now, all they got is yours." The teacher took over and held the floor. "Yeah, well, I told him we had to talk. I said, 'What's wrong with this picture? I'm paying bills every month and you're not putting anything down on the table.' He said, 'Honey, I just thought you could handle things.' I said, 'Sure I can. But if I have to, why do I need you?' Check this out. The man asked me what I wanted for Christmas and I told him I wanted this emerald ring I saw." She raised her left hand, flexing her index finger to show it off. "It was only $250. The man brought me this big box Christmas morning and it was some pantsuits. Yeah. Can you believe that? I said, 'What do I need with more pantsuits?' He said, 'Honey, I just wanted you to look good.' Humph! I said, 'This is *not* working.' He's my fifth one, but I'm divorcing him, too." Silence. "Maybe you just keep marryin' somebody else's husband," said her consoling friend.

The women's talk was like a bite of fatback when you are on a salt-free diet. It brought back some of the tastier memories that seasoned my youth in Jacksonville, just a couple of hours north of Zora's town. We had a kind of theater on the streets every day. A simple "hello" became a verbal volley of improvised dialogue punctuated with body language. For instance, two men walking in opposite directions meet on the street and greet each other without breaking stride:

First Passerby: My man! (*Rears back head as if startled*)

Second Passerby: What it is! (*Slides palm across friend's hand and pumps a handshake*)

First Passerby: You got it. (*Swings a playful punch at friend's shoulder and backs away*)

Second Passerby: Doing it to death.

First Passerby: I know that's right. If I'm lyin,' I'm flyin.' (*They back away from each other, speaking loudly, in unison*)

Both: Later.

We did not do much reading, though, which is why I got around to Zora so late. And even if we had been readers, there was a paucity of black female voices we knew about, especially southerners and Florida girls. I had to learn to pursue books over the years on my own; still, even now I feel a bit love-starved. A call from a new friend the other day really brought it into focus for me. We had not talked in several months, and he had news he hoped would bring us closer together. The relationship so far had faltered in the cracks between our sensibilities. I was a black writer who loved making music. He was a black businessman who loved money-making schemes. We joked about our differences of culture and history, an impassable gulf. Opportunities he took for granted in his urban, middle-class life came much later for us poorer southern cousins. With little else to talk about, our conversations were usually superficial—and brief.

The familiar huskiness of his voice spiraled up through the phone and into my ear. "Guess what?" it purred with promise. He had started reading again, he said. Mostly nonfiction books. He named an author, and his tone arched with surprise when the name was unfamiliar to me. "Finding the time is difficult, but I'm actually doing it," he said. Imagine that. Finally, I thought, the written word was getting through to him. "Tell me something," he said, and the teacher in me perked up, ready for some intellectual sparring of ideas. "What's the best book you've read lately?" I did not feel the blow coming, but I sure felt it hit me, hard. I fumbled for an answer. My brain clicked back at least a year to retrieve the memory of just one book read in its entirety. "I don't *know*," I struck back with feigned impatience when I could not even remember a title. Quickly, I changed the subject and soon ended the call. But the truth was out; it was time for me to confess. I love books, but I am an unfaithful reader. There, I said it. Admitting the problem is the first step toward recovery.

I am not sure exactly when my stamina began to wane. It probably had a lot to do with so many years of writing for a daily newspaper, where the appetite for words is voracious. The more that words went out of me, the fewer that came in, and as the years progressed, I must have developed the book-collecting habit as an antidote. Four shelves—all I can handle right now—overflow with hardcovers and paperbacks I have purchased new and rescued from sidewalk sales and discount racks. I peruse catalogs and send in orders like a lonely man looking for mail-order brides. Stories by Chinese, East Indian, Hispanic, Filipino, and Native American writers are propped beside classics, popular fiction, anthologies of black writers from the twenties to the nineties, and, of course, a collection of James Baldwin. I show each of them reverence by not even writing my name inside the cover, and I guard them jealously, preferring to give one away rather than loan it, for fear it will never be returned. Tips of bookmarks peek up from at least ten of these books—relationships started over time but interrupted. Fortunately, these friends are not fickle; they will wait patiently for me to come back to them again.

Name the excuse for not reading, and I have used it at one time or another. Too busy. Too tired. Aging eyes. I read for my work, so who has time to read for pleasure anymore? I teach writing and literature now, and those books have to be read closely for academic study. Surely, that counts for something. But deep down I know it is not the same as reading for love. *Real* reading is a book that keeps a person up until 2:00 A.M., vowing to quit after just one more chapter. It makes someone actually prefer staying at home to going out with friends. It conjures up characters who visit people's dreams and dialogue that pops up in their conversations. I know the feeling. I was smitten young. Growing up an only child, I was placated with Baby Ruths and Butterfingers and books as safe companions. If I came home right after school, stayed inside and out of trouble, I was allowed to stay up as late as I wanted to read.

During my rebellious teenage years, books eventually caused me to run away from home. The outside influences seeped into my psyche subtly. It started quite innocently with my tenth-grade English teacher, "old Miz Griffin," as we called her. We had to do two book reports a week in her class, each one both verbal and written. She was munchkin-sized and had a stare that pinned me to a wall like a thumbtack when she asked me a question. She nailed me one Friday afternoon as I squirmed to defend my report on a book I had selected from the meager offerings at our school library. I had only read the book jacket, and she knew it. She had such high expectations of me, she said, which deeply wounded my pride. Soon after that, I got my first public library card from outside the neighborhood and fell for the writings of James Baldwin. I remember the circumstances of our introduction vividly.

It was on one of my first visits to the mammoth "white" library once it was integrated. Every Saturday I took the bus downtown, perused the fiction shelves, and pulled out novels, doing a Geiger-counter scan of the first pages until I found one that compelled me to read on. The affinity with Baldwin was instant. I was going through a period of Baptist church-choir-singing fervor, and he enticed me into the world of the child evangelist in *Go Tell It on the Mountain*. Later I learned that much of the material in his fiction was autobiographical, and I was hooked. Baldwin whisked me off to strange lands that fueled my imagination—to France and Switzerland, where he had lived for several years in self-exile. He was black, yet universal in his approach to human relations, writing about racial injustice for a largely white audience. He also wrote tenderly about the specific emotional conflicts caused by his feelings of "otherness" as a homosexual, but it was the desire for intimacy inherent in all of us that he conveyed. I was too young then to understand everything he wrote, but after reading five of his books in a row, I knew two things, both of which came true: I would one day be a writer and I would visit Europe.

After Baldwin I developed a taste for strong, combative characters, perhaps to compensate for the timid introspective life I led then. I read the bold adventure-seekers of Edna Ferber's epic westerns one week and the deadly wit of the British Iris Murdoch the next. The pattern was set, and even throughout college between books by Sartre, Camus, and Chaucer, I managed to sneak in *Peyton Place* and *Gone with the Wind*. But it was not until I curled up with the brash southern slang of Hurston that I knew I had come home. She captured a rhythm of life and people I found familiar, although much of that flavor has long since disappeared. The anvil-slinging, melody-humming, hardworking railroad men. The loose-talking, knife-carrying, hardscrabble juke-joint women. The black and white sides of Florida towns. Her words stirred up many memories.

In much the same way, I have had to piece together fragments of stories about my past to give that little two-year-old girl in the photograph a heritage and to create for myself a history. The stories I tell as a writer reflect bits and pieces of who I am. The act of writing itself has been a process of awakening and discovery. I started writing as a teenager because of conflicting emotions. I wrote mean-spirited poems about the girls in school who all had boyfriends when I did not. I wrote about the terrors of being left at home alone. None of it was writing that I shared or saved, but I needed my ego stroked. I discovered I could get attention, even from people I might never meet. I once wrote an impassioned letter to the movie star Janet Leigh after reading a fan magazine about her perfect marriage to Tony Curtis and their two perfect daughters, Jamie Lee and Kelly. I wrote to her about my overweight insecurities and my dreams of escaping my hometown. On small, dainty stationery, she responded with a typed, five-page letter of commiseration, telling me how she had lost weight and changed her life. She was the first person to tell me that I could change mine.

Nobody else I knew was a writer, but folks swapped stories about other people's lives, and I listened. In Jacksonville's summers, we opened the windows and battled the heat with cardboard fans. We lived a front-porch life. The grown-ups would sit long into the night as the cars whizzed by, telling what they jokingly called "colored stories." Every community has a rhythm to which children are especially attuned, and in mine the drone of hard times was dominant. But these tales, tinged with the storyteller's peculiar version of life's truths, always had a raunchy-sweet rift to it. On rare evenings, I managed to wrangle a late hour outside before bedtime with the women. As they clamped their daughters hard between their knees for a hair braiding, one of them was sure to start an uproarious dressing down of some man for doing her wrong or of some woman for trying to break up her home. Afterward, every time I saw the subject of these anecdotes in public, my view of him or her was tainted by that tidbit of inside information, which was the point, of course. Women swapped stories during midweek choir practices and Saturday fish fries at church and after Sunday evening service when almost everyone was gone. The older church sisters clucked over reports of the latest escapade by some lapsed Christian or nonbeliever, careful to paint in all the vivid details, but only because the tale proved that the sinner needed to come to God.

During one of those front-porch sessions, I overheard the one about Miss Harriet. We roomed with her for awhile upstairs over a pool hall, on a street where men shopped for clothes and women and fought over both. On the kitchen windowsill, Miss Harriet kept a water glass filled with green water that I was always admonished never to touch. Inside the glass, a long, thin, black strand bobbed up and down. The potion, I learned after we moved, came from a root worker who could cast spells for luck and mix up charms for love. He had told her to put one of her boyfriend's pubic hairs in the jar of dark, thick liquid. As long as the hair stayed in there and grew, he remained with her. "Six kids, and still in love," Miss Harriet used to declare proudly, as her boyfriend grinned like a jack-in-the-box clown. Now that was a story too good for me not to repeat.

Whenever the women gathered to gossip, a story about white people always provided grist for the mill. They often gleaned information from the daily news. "Girl, did you read about that man who killed his whole family? Children, too!" the storyteller began. "No!" "Sure did. Poisoned them. Fell over right there, eating dinner." "Lord have mercy," the listener commiserated. "White or black?" When the storyteller reached this point, the tale took off in one of two directions. If the subject was black, the women dissected the specifics of the case. "Was that over behind Eighth Street Pharmacy? That's a bad corner there. Always something happening." If they knew the people or their families, even vaguely, they made some assessment of their psychological shortcomings. "All those 'blankety-blanks' got something wrong with them. It's a shame." "Uh-huh," the chorus would affirm. If the subject of the story was white, the script was less analytical. "I tell you, those people are sick," someone said, and someone else concurred. "Uh-h-h-huh. They'll do anything." "That's right." "You don't catch black people acting like that." Of course, our firsthand knowledge of whites was limited, and misperceptions about others tend to thrive when people are isolated. Whites were strange people who acted weirdly, and the best thing to do was to stay away from them. That was the moral to the stories that unnerved me most as a child.

I was chewing on the knuckle of a pickled pig foot while scanning the comic strips for *Beetle Bailey* and *Mary Worth* one day, and Mama was reading one of her black news magazines, when I heard her gasp like a gas stove ready to light. My ears perked up, but at that point it could have been anything—something she read, an errand she forgot, some trouble for me. I did not look up. Then the clucking sound started, tongue slapping the roof of her mouth, followed by, "Lord, have mercy. I can't believe it." That meant it was really bad. I was almost afraid to hear. Mama had her tortoise-shell eyeglasses in one hand and massaged the cluster of moles across the bridge of her nose with the other. She shook her head sadly. Oh, this was really good, I could tell. I tried to sound cool about it. "What is it, Mama?" "Read this," she said. She handed me the magazine. "It's just unbelievable what those people will do." The vivid details stayed glued in my memory all these years. In a neighborhood somewhere up north, two young black girls had been going door to door selling cookies when a white man coerced them inside his home. According to the police, the girls had been sexually molested; the culprit, a Doberman, following the depraved instructions of his owner. I added strange white men, Dobermans, and door-to-door solicitations to my list of things to be afraid of and to avoid.

I started telling stories of my own in high school, not yet writing them down. Once, my friend Janice went out on a limb to get me into a new social club some of the Miss-Its were forming. The group decided that I was qualified to attend the membership meeting because I was going to college. "I'll have to see," I said, stalling. The disappointment that rose in Janice's eyes unsettled me. I debated. Should I make up some complicated story, or should I tell her the truth? We just could not afford the monthly five-dollar dues or the material for the official club outfit. I was leaning toward the truth when mischief lit up her face. "Is it Ken-n-ny?" She dragged out the syllables of his name in a teasing way. I had thrown away the chain with the ring attached that once hung around my neck, but I still felt a tug of embarrassment from the story I had once made up that even now she would not let me forget. I had been sick and tired of Janice boasting about her boyfriend, so I fought back in the only way I knew. One day I found a senior class ring under a hedge while I was walking to school. It was obviously a male's—several sizes too large for any of my fingers—with the insignia of a school across town and the intriguing initials "K.G." By the time I reached homeroom that morning, I had created "Kenny." He was two years older than me, nice-looking but not a pretty boy. He had joined the army right out of high school and wrote me love letters from the places where he traveled. For weeks Janice pestered me and I basked in the attention. "Did you get a letter from Kenny?" she nagged. "Let me see one, please," she begged. Of course, I never had one in my purse at the time. Then her suspicions turned into goading. "I'll bet there aren't any letters. Are there? Are there?" We even stopped speaking to each other for a few days over her insult to my feigned integrity. Confession time came in a moment of reconciliation, when she told me she had broken up with her boyfriend. I admitted it. "All right. There is no Kenny. OK?" Tears now stung my eyes on the heels of having to duck out of the club. Janice, a budding bean pole, giggled with retribution. I had mine in mind. By gym class the next day, a new story had circulated, this one with *my* budding knack for embroidery. "Janice is so skinny she stuffs socks in her bra . . . and in her panties for hips. And they fell out yesterday . . . from under her dress . . . in assembly!" Janice cringed. Our friendship almost ended. She complained loudly, but my mother just shook her head wearily. "That child of mine will tell anything." Sitting there, head back, listening on the charter bus, I chuckled to myself at the memory.

The teacher's story about her husband had riveted me, and I wanted to hear more, but unfortunately, everyone else on the bus was getting in one last doze. So I indulged myself a little more:

> *I can just imagine Zora on a drive around Eatonville. . . . Her stylish marcelled hair is ironed flat and crimped like creases in greasy tin foil. Her feathered hat is cocked to the side—a lopsided crown with an exclamation point. Lake Sybelle's breeze tastes like cigarettes and gin as her red convertible whizzes by with men telling her stories, telling her lies. The live oaks rustle. Look out. Zora's back home again. "Girl, you sho is sump'n," croons one of the men with calloused hands and sweaty arms she scooped up from some railroad work site for a sunset country ride. "You better watch yo'self 'round here." The driver rears back her head like a stallion tossing off its bit and increases her speed. "I ain't gotta do nuthin,' honey, but stay black and die." The roar of the engine swallows her laughter as she rounds the curve.*

As we pulled into town beneath streamers emblazoned with Zora's name lining four blocks of the two-lane main street of town, I marveled at the way time brings about a change. The townsfolk in her day might not have appreciated the writer's folksy, earthy portrayals of them, but today's Eatonville capitalizes on her notoriety at least once a year. Collections of her books sold fast at the filling station turned into a fine-arts museum that was named after her. The director who staged one of her folklore plays featuring Negro work songs and spirituals deadpanned that she felt she had become "one of the vessels" of the Zora spirit.

Rain was predicted, announced one of the organizers, but "we just

Zora Neale Hurston. Photo by Carl Van Vechten, 1935.

Zora-Nealed it," adopting the attitude that will could overpower nature. Of course, the rain backed down. The celebrity host for the night explained the noted writer this way: "Zora said what she thought and never apologized for what she did." He received a Plexiglass paperweight award, dubbed "a Zora," for his participation. I half expected some pajama-clad, turban-wearing, African-princess-pretending character like the one Hurston reportedly sometimes conjured up to make a grand surprise entrance claiming to be "Zora, the Outrageous," incarnate. But Hurston was serious about her interest in other cultures, doing research in Haiti and parts of the Caribbean. She liked nothing better than observing. The outdoor Sunday festival looked fittingly like an African bazaar. Testy

Yoruban and Cameroon jewelry merchants chased away sticky-fingered children and amateur photographers. ("No picture, no sale. No sale, no picture.") Vendors hawked hats shaped like Frisbees, only giant-sized and warped, and evening dresses and three-piece suits made of dashiki and kinte cloths. Word of chitlin dinners on sale at a nearby church shot through the crowd like a lighted match on a gasoline leak. By the time business returned to normal, the barbecue and fried-fish peddlers had to reignite their coals.

A sign on the gazebo near the entrance to the festival caught my eye: "Zora's Special Places Tour." Finally, I thought, a chance to get the real story. "I'm your 'Local Zora,'" announced the tour guide, as the trolley bounced out of the parking lot onto the main street. We were on our way to view the landmarks that Zora had described in a historical guide to Florida. "As you can see, I've dressed the part." The tour guide stood up, lifted her jacket, and did a three-quarter turn, asking us to picture stately Zora, short and plump in a rhinestone cap and a low-cut body suit. I refused. The tour passed the Sewell house and the Macedonia AME Church, landmarks—still intact—that Zora had once described in the magazine. It followed her route circling Lake Sybelle, where she and her men friends had gone for raucous rides, and traveled out of Eatonville to the Maitland Art Center, the former home of artist and arts patron Andre Smith. He died in 1959, a year before Zora. "They say his ghost wanders the courtyard from October through April, the time of the year he used to spend here," explained a docent standing in the courtyard at the center. As we filed out, the Local Zora filled us in. "Zora used to come here to meditate. And they wrote letters to each other, but they were lost in a fire at the art school across the street where he lived. The public was never allowed in there. They say there might have been something going on." She winked. We climbed back on board the trolley. I continued to mull over her words:

> I can imagine Zora at Andre Smith's house. . . .
>
> A carving of Christ gazes serenely from the rust-red stone pillars upon the lone visitor who waits quietly in the open-air chapel. "Writing is going slow," Zora tells Andre. He understands, he says. They stroll in silence through the courtyard of his artists' retreat in all-white Maitland under the stone-carved glare of devils and Mayan warriors. Sagging branches sigh over the easel where his latest painting of the folks in Eatonville dries.

(Top) In the courtyard of what was once the house of artist and arts patron Andre Smith. (Bottom) Andre Smith's home, now Maitland Art Center.

Her bravado breaks down. "It's so hard making ends meet." "You know I'll always help," he says. Gently, he guides her across the road to his private quarters. First, they must have four o'clock tea and talk about her work.

As we reached the part of town where Hurston had dreamed herself beyond Eatonville, I paid close attention. I wanted to see the yard where she saw "visions" that became prophecies of her future, the house where she flagged down strangers to give her a ride up the road as far as she could see, and farther—"past the horizon." Here, her mother encouraged her to be bold and adventurous and "jump the sun." The tour stopped in front of the town fire station, and we got off to look at a misshapen boulder that looked like gray driftwood. Inserted in the boulder was a plaque with an inscription citing the writer's birth and death. That was all. My expectations sank. The Local Zora rushed over with ebullience again. "Zora's friend's house *used* to be here, and when she came to town, she would have to sneak in and she'd stay here," we were told. A few yards away, where Zora's house once stood, was a field large enough for an apartment complex. A bar and lounge painted a brooding charcoal color overlooked the empty lot with a defiantly playful graffiti sign on one side of the building. The name of the place, scrawled boldly on the sign, was one word: "Heroes." Joe Clark's store, which Hurston immortalized as the heartbeat of the town, where the men gathered on the front porch until dark swapping stories and lies, used to be just across the street. A building stood there, but the name had been changed and the porch was gone. It was now an Asian-owned grocery store.

On the road again, our tour guide explained that she was a member of the black students' group at Rollins College in Winter Park, the group that had donated a stone with Hurston's name on it to the school's Walk of Fame in 1987. And like me, she had a personal homage she longed to pay. She described a historical redesign of her hometown she had created for her master's thesis, "something sort of like an all-American town square, but Greek, with columns, and enclosed," where the townsfolk could gather for meetings and celebrations. But the town was not interested. The lightbulb seemed to dim on her spirit. As the tour pulled back into the parking lot and the trolley shuddered to a stop, she stayed seated, nodding goodbye as the customers debarked, barely acknowledging the occasional dollar bill dropped into the tip jar. I hung around, sensing that she had more to tell. "People just have no vision," she said, neatly reordering her notes for the next tour. She tapped the stack of papers firmly on the seat for emphasis. "They persecuted Zora. They persecuted the prophet Jeremiah. They're persecuting me. I'll probably have to die like Zora before I'm known."

> *I can imagine Zora, in the end, alone. . . . "Who'd believe it? My own people. My own people." The residents of the women's home are used to the sleepless late-night sounds. She can be quite a sight, too. Coarse, graying hair carelessly pinned. Sunken eyes. The same frayed white maid's uniform worn to work every day. Zora lies on her single bed in the shadow of the lamp on the nightstand, the headlines from the black press swirling around in her tired mind, replaying her infamy. "Writer Charged . . . ," "Mother of 10-Year-Old Says . . . ," "Molested . . . ," ". . . Out of Country When . . . ," ". . . Cleared Today." She rubs her heavy legs to ease the ache from being on her feet all day. No writing today. No one wants to publish it anyway. Her head throbs, and she tries to forget the lies that should never have been told.*

The writer was not popular with the black literati of the thirties and forties. She wrote plays, folklore, fiction, and essays, and she was too good at self-promotion and endearing herself to whites. Richard Wright called her a "handkerchief head," among other things. A mother who felt she had been insulted by Hurston falsely charged the writer with molesting her son. The writer was out of the country at the time the assault allegedly happened, and proved it, but the damage had been done.

"I am *pleased* with my purchases!" One voice squealed above the rest of the women on the bus as it waded through the festival traffic and headed out of town. "Can you believe it? Five dollars a yard." The squealer stretched out a panel of abstract African print for group appraisal and held it to her chest with her chin. Shopping bags bulged with souvenir posters and oil paintings of African griots in blue or in a rose-colored scheme. One woman licked the last of "the best barbecue sauce in town" off the tips of her fingers, refusing to share. "I've got somebody I want you to meet," said the club member who had made the introductions. She was standing next to my seat, pushing another woman's chest forward toward my face. "This is our writer-friend," she said to her. The woman looked to be in her fifties, eyeglasses low and pinched tight on her nose like a schoolmarm calling her class to order. She smiled, and a shade went up in her eyes. "I hear you're interested in Miss Hurston. She was my teacher in school in Fort Pierce just before she died." I left Zoraville disappointed because I had not learned as much as I had hoped about the real life of the writer. Now, I was finally meeting a person who actually *knew* something.

Scooting over, I cleared room on the seat next to me. I had so many questions. What was she like? Did she talk about her writing? Did she really die penniless, with a broken heart? The schoolmarm waited patiently until I finished rattling off my list. Out of breath, I waited for her answers. "She was our substitute and what I remember is—" Yes? "—that she was . . . different. Very different." How did she look? "Tall, not big. And not well-dressed. Not pretty, but she had a way about her. That's why we remembered her." What kind of way? "The way she talked. We used to laugh at her because she spoke so . . . differently. When she talked she used such flowery words." And? She shrugged. "That's all I remember." More bits and pieces. I gave up on ever knowing the whole story.

The mood of the bus downshifted to serious. Instinctively, we started making preparations for the resumption of our regular lives. Some of the women cleaned up the peanut shells and candy wrappers from their junk-food binge. Others dabbed on powder or fresh coats of lipstick. We pulled out our carry-on baggage again so that we could get to it easily. The same women who had left like truants, eagerly shedding their responsibilities, dutifully lined up at phone booths during the last rest stop to call home. I felt a little sorry to see the pilgrimage end. I had missed these grits-and-gravy, tall-tale-telling voices that reminded me of my youth. Sometimes that past seems more like somebody else's story now, and I am just the researcher and transcriber. I guess that is why I have this fascination with Zora-telling. She was a product of her time, with its migration of blacks from the rural South to the cities, the promise of prosperity, the flowering of black writers in Harlem. The stories she told were her sense of place, of culture, of identity. As she branched out from home, she held firmly to her roots. But Zora Neale Hurston was also a segregationist, conservative in her views, believing that separate was equal. She may have been in the minority in the black community in her time, but she certainly was not alone in thinking that we had it good and should just shut up and stay put. I am a product of my time, too—a time of black migration from the restrictions of segregation to the opportunities of the white mainstream. In one generation we moved from beer joints to wine bars, from pigs' feet to sushi, from the poverty line to the middle class. Still, there is a longing for a sense of place, of culture, of permanence, of identity that continues to elude me.

I closed my eyes, but I could tell that heads nodded in empathy with the voices in front of me. They talked about hometowns, and the main speaker was a Florida-born woman like many of us. "I was nineteen, and we had just got married and moved to Panama City in Florida's northwest panhandle. They told me to ride in the back of the bus, and I said, 'Why?' I always sat in the front." *I don't blame you, girl!* "I mean, at home we had our *own* buses. Blacks were the only ones who rode the bus, so we had it to ourselves." *I know, that's right!* "We had our own society and there was a lot of good in it, but integration killed all that. Heck, I didn't even know I was black until I got married and moved." *Sure 'nough. I hear you.* Even I could identify to a certain extent. Without realizing it, for the first time in a long, long while I was not aware of being black either on this trip with these women in Zoraville. But I was also aware that I was not really one of them. I was their "writer-friend." Maybe some of us just arrive in this world with a passport stamped "foreigner." No matter where we travel, we find we never quite fit in. So we piece together a life of meeting people, going places, collecting stories. And the journey we are on starts to make a little more sense.

SECOND COMINGS OF AGE

*T*he rust brown deer perpetually grazes in sparse grass on a hilltop, attentive against a clear beige sky. The front legs, thin and fragile, are planted firmly on the ground, but the hind legs are bent with the impulse to run. Actually, it is just a three-by-six-foot rug stitched with washable acrylic yarn, suitable for any indoor living space. But I could never bring myself to lay it on a floor. Its wintery scene is too pleasantly diametrical to my tropical surroundings in South Florida, the texture too fragile to be trampled upon. The piece is one of those few possessions with meaning that has traveled with me through all the years of taking on and letting go. I have kept only a couple of things in my life longer: the turquoise birthstone ring from my first and only surprise birthday party, at sixteen, and a dog-eared collection of Shakespeare's comedies and tragedies from college days. Louise, a longtime friend of mine, made the deer rug when she was in transition. She also made one for herself that hangs in her home. Her life was in turmoil, her values uprooted, and I commiserated from the smug distance of a woman twelve years younger who did not know, or did not want to believe, that her turn would surely come one day.

Louise had been married to Mitch for twelve years when we met through work in the 1970s. She was in her mid-thirties—short, pixieish, and full of mischief—and I liked her instantly. Once she showed me a picture of herself at the age of twenty-one—blonde hair long and fine, midway down her back, which gave her a fragile, young Mia Farrow look. "He was older than me and I looked up to him. I thought he was so sophisticated," she said with the past tense in her voice. I had been a witness to one end of some of their verbal brawls because her desk was just a few feet from mine. Often she slammed down the phone, exasperated. Sometimes she almost cried. In calmer moments she rationalized, "At least it's never dull with him." One night, a few years into our friendship, as we sat chatting on the orange Danish modern sofa in the house my husband and I had just bought, she suddenly turned to me with a sober look. "If I didn't love you so much, I'd be jealous of you," she said. I tried to laugh it off, although it did unnerve me a little. I was pregnant and happy, if not always content. The end of their relationship began when they agreed to divorce, but still it turned into a long, expensive, ugly fight. Subpoenas over the sale of stocks, the house, and the sailboat kept coming for many months after the decree was granted. The stress took its medical toll on her nervous system, sapped her strength, and forced her to reorder her priorities. At forty, Louise found a quiet man her age; she married him, and they escaped South Florida for the rural life. In a lounge chair in their home in the mountains that rim the Shenandoah Valley, she sat and knitted and learned to wait. It took some time after her second marriage for the financial settlement from the divorce to become final and for her to slam the door shut on the first half of her life. With steady sweeps of the needle—day in, day out—she hooked and looped and shaped the deer tapestry.

I did not have the heart to tell her that it never quite suited the stark white wall above the orange Danish modern sofa where I first hung it, out of respect more than admiration. The traditional look conflicted with my contemporary female tastes. The women's movement took off in the seventies, and I was an eager recipient of its benefits. While still in my twenties, I married, forged a career, started a family, and considered myself terminally unique. I was one of those women who came of age with arro-

The deer tapestry.

gance, and I felt sorry for stay-at-home women like Louise—women who seemed to have no ambition of their own, as I did, to change the world. But sometimes on nights when the house was silent, I could feel restriction and doubt tugging at me as I entered my thirties. A mortgage. School-aged children. Stiff competition at work. Insecurities. A nagging sense of wanting something different, something more. Relationships usually end long before we leave them. Vainly, the heart avoids what the instinct knows is true. As my children reached their teens, outgrowing the nest, I was the one who flew. I was forty when I said goodbye to the house with the orange Danish modern sofa and to my husband. I took some old photos, a few books, some Richie Havens and Bob Marley records, a somber-looking pastel portrait of me in my twenties, and, for some odd reason, the deer scene.

It was the first thing I hung for comfort in my dreary one-bedroom apartment. The incongruous brown on the purple wall matched my erratic moods. I spent many nights there, free but miserable, alone, using too much vodka to drown my indecision about where to go next with my life. Fear can be a great paralyzer; sobriety, a mobilizer. When I moved to a bungalow, finally, with resolutions to begin building once more, the deer dominated a khaki-colored bedroom wall of my new home and gave the room a cozy feel. I hung white lace curtains and assembled bookcases to line each living-room wall. And I began to write—until three or four in the morning if I wanted—listening to jazz tunes and just a little bit of blues. Now the deer hangs in a stylish new home in a rare quiet corner of urban sprawl, still close enough to the action of the city. But it is a place I seem to always be leaving. In the process of making transitions and rediscoveries, I unearthed a gene for wandering.

It may have been inherited, programmed before birth by my father's longings, or perhaps just a memory embedded deep in a restless childhood soul. Even in the closely guarded southern black world of my youth, I occasionally rebelled by veering from the path that had been laid out for me. Sometimes on my way home from elementary school during a brief stay in the projects, I deliberately walked past the complex where those "rough people" lived—the people I was supposed to avoid—and I played imaginary hopscotch along the sidewalks that snaked through that part of the projects, drawing out the game. I took slow, measured jumps, sneaking looks at the forbidden. I remember, even at that young age, staring hard at those look-alike walls and windows, the same as ours, trying to get a peek into strangers' lives. As I got a little older, my mother sent me off to the downtown heart of the city to the movies on Saturdays and holidays with the warning to stay safely on the outskirts of "the blocks" as it was called. Of course, I figured out a way to venture off. On the first leg of the bus ride I stopped at Krystal's for a ten-cent special hamburger before the double-feature matinee. Inching up in the black line, I had to be careful not to brush against an arm or back of the whites who sat at the counter while I waited. I shoveled down my meal by the time the short ride with my transfer was over, and then I stepped out on Ashley and Davis streets, the area I was supposed to avoid.

I remember one day figuring that I would just take a quick stroll—three blocks, in and out. I bounced on the balls of my tennis shoes, trying to give a rhythm to my walk that would merge with the beat of the street, trying to look like I fit in. At two outdoor tables heaped with cheap shirts and underwear, several women raced through the merchandise as if they were digging for gold. I scooted past just in time, as one woman's elbow landed a jab into the other's rib cage, escaping the fight that erupted over a yellow Ban Lon stretch top. A record store blasted "Yakkety-yak, don't talk back" from a 45 on the turntable. A group of teenage boys circled the record player, singing along instead of buying. One of them caught a look at me as I passed the door, and I slowed down, trying to bounce up a little taller. Near the end of the line of stores, some men lounged against a brick building beneath a neon bar sign, with looks that gave me too much scrutiny. As they swigged drinks from paper bags, they slurred their words and hurled them at me. I did not understand what they said, but I knew they were words I was not supposed to hear. *Watch out for old men,* my mother had warned. Fear spread from my heart to my legs and did not disappear until I rounded the corner out of their sight, relieved. In the comforting dark of the Strand theater, for the next five hours I could safely escape. There, in films, a much larger world first beckoned. It took me more than thirty years to answer the call.

The longing begins soon after New Year's, seeping into my conversations with friends. "So where are you traveling next?" they want to know. Their vicarious bags are packed and ready, and it becomes my job to feed their insatiable escape fantasies. Those are the fantasies triggered by a stressful workday, a boring relationship, or an accumulation of the irritations of daily life; the fantasies that a family or business trip cannot appease; the dreams of an exotic getaway that disintegrates into migraines by the time two busy people can finally agree on a date and place.

I have been through all of those scenarios at various stages in my life. As an unmarried woman, however, a different challenge surfaced: how do I learn to play by myself? I have spent years learning how to live that way, now that I am an "aloneable" woman. That is what I call those of us who are alone and able to envision a time when that will change but who choose to lead the single life right now. It is a finely distinguished group, different from the male-bashers and the husband-hunters; we are older, trying to be wiser next time around. For some, this is a time used for healing and professional exploration; for others, spiritual and personal growth or recovery. We are trying to plant our own roots firmly in new ground. The first time I visited my friend Louise, the knitter, in her new home in the Shenandoah Valley, she wanted me to see the fall leaves changing colors. We drove slowly up the steep winding curves of Skyline Drive, stopping at lookout points along the way. When I breathe deeply, I can still taste the crispness of that Virginia air. "Life is pretty dull here compared to the fun we used to have in Florida," she told me as we stopped at one point to survey the vastness below us. "But I like it that way." Hooking elbows, we walked back to the car to head home, and it was obvious that her life had finally become a comfortable fit. So has mine. Instead of trying to have it all, I have learned to settle for less stressful work, less money, and a little more free time and solitude. I have learned to dine, travel, and go out on Saturday nights alone, ready at any moment to enjoy company again.

In the past eight years or so, I have hit most of the major cities in the United States and Canada. With just two carry-on bags and a foreign phrase book, I have made five transatlantic crossings. I have fought off airsickness in a bush plane soaring above the peaks of Denali, and my fingers have nearly frozen on the top slopes of the Matterhorn. In a tiny crypt of a room in Venice, I once burned incense to ward off the rancid smell of a "scenic" brackish green canal. I spent an hour circling downtown Rome, lost like an aging street urchin, until a kindly waiter took me by the hand and led the way to my hotel. My friends marvel that I always travel to these unfamiliar places solo. But other women feed *my* fantasies—the ones who tromp through jungles, jump from airplanes, ride freighters, or live in tents and huts. We all test ourselves in different ways.

I tell my friends that I want to try a camera safari or a stay in one foreign country for several weeks to see how well I can survive—*as soon as I get the nerve,* I mutter under my breath. I probably will not tell them that on every one of my journeys, at some point, I retreat to my room for a few hours, overwhelmed. I just lie there in a new, unfamiliar bed with

On a trip through the Shenandoah Valley.

the covers over my head, but only for a little while, because I am too curious about what I will discover about myself once I go outside my comfort zone again. Over the years, I have begun to realize that I often feel more at home walking the streets of foreign cities than I do in my everyday world. Voices dart in and out all around me in different languages, but I am immune to their meaning except for a few basic words. People may stare at me sometimes. Swathed in my shawls with hats and slinky skirts instead of the T-shirt-and-sneakers tourist uniform, I am just another dark-skinned stranger in their midst. Driving through some small southern towns might cause me more trepidation.

Still, I admit that when I hear an American voice, I perk up. It is easy to get quickly acquainted, but I usually end up spending more time talking with an English-speaker who is from another country. If I encounter another southerner, however, I should know by now that making the acquaintance usually leads us somewhere else. One afternoon in Seville, I was reminded of the bond, the stranglehold. The stifling mid-afternoon summer heat had sent most of Seville indoors until dinnertime. I was just glad to take off my sweater for awhile. After spending the first half of the day on a bus, touring the city and shivering in air-conditioned temperatures that seemed to dip by the hour, I was eager for some warm-weather time alone. Early on in the three-hour trip from Malaga, I had noticed a white American man whose booming voice and southern twang were a disturbing taste of home. That sound was the roar of pickup trucks, the rattle of gun racks, the mouths that twisted sideways and spat out, "Hey, gal" and "Hey, nigger" to me in the same malicious tone. It conjured up instant stay-away memories. So I had attached myself instead to the only other black woman among the twenty or so English-speaking people in the group. During one stop at a cathedral, we struck up a conversation. She was from Washington, D.C., she said, visiting Spain with a friend. A young white woman within earshot heard her comment and introduced herself as being from D.C. as well. And it turned out that they were vacationing in resorts near each other. Quicker than I could snap a picture, the two women connected and sauntered off like Siamese twins, with me, the outsider, trying to wedge myself between them. By the time we stopped for some free time at a plaza, I had given them up for a bench in the sun. A chorus of Spanish-speaking voices babbled around me, South-Florida style. I relaxed, content with the brief respite from tourist sites, when from the corner of my eye I caught sight of the man with the twang heading toward me. I braced myself for what was coming.

He had overheard me earlier talking about my work collecting oral histories of people in South Florida who shared their race-relations experiences. The book was already finished, but still he wanted to tell me *his* memories. He was a successful businessman living in a wealthy, racially mixed suburb of Central Florida, but he had been born and raised in a place nearby that I knew as a speed-trap stop on a highway between Jacksonville and Gainesville. The rare times that I had taken that route by car it was with windows raised, doors locked, and breath held until I had safely passed. He talked with urgency, unable to stay seated, telling me about a frightening experience in 1968 when he was thirteen and had disobeyed his mother to sneak into a field to watch a flag-waving, anti-school-integration rally held by the Klan. He talked about an eye-opening trip to Williamsburg, Virginia, where he realized for the first time that blacks had a long history of living and working in this country but had received unfair treatment. Other whites had changed people like him, he said, by challenging the attitudes he had been taught. Hunched down, he talked about the racial name-calling that he had once considered normal. His arms swept the air with wide gestures as he flung the "n-word" around, making the point of how freely it was used then. My ears stung like whips from cattails as I steeled myself to listen. I was aware that the sprinkling of Spaniards sitting within earshot were turning and staring; the intensity of the conversation must have been obvious, even if they did not grasp the content. And I was glad they did not. If this encounter had happened just about anywhere in America, it might have drawn a crowd and a reaction—possibly a physical altercation.

I had endured painful listening to harsh words and troubling incidents told by other people I had interviewed. I had learned to park my emotions while the veterans of racial conflict bared their wounds. Writing it down was a challenge, because I had to try to tell both sides of the story— black and white—when I had lived only one version. And I was still trying to figure out how to capture those feelings on paper; even today they continue to be fresh in my mind. The trip to Spain was supposed to be a respite, my chance to escape, to rest, to unwind and forget about race matters for awhile. But the Florida man reminded me that the time for telling our stories and for listening never ends, at least not for southerners. When I spotted the returning "Siamese twins," I felt a sudden uneasiness. He must have felt it, too, because he stopped himself in mid-sentence. We exchanged business cards, and I pulled my sweater close around my shoulders again as we climbed back on the tour bus through separate doors.

Sometimes when I travel, I feel apologetic when I mention that I was born in Florida and that I never left. It sounds so limiting. For most people in other parts of the world, the state has a one-dimensional "sun-and-fun" image, with some Latin and Caribbean flavor tossed in for a little color. A strange thing has happened: the more cosmopolitan the South Florida area has become, the more we natives—both black and white—have surfaced as an ethnic group of our own. We seek each other out by our drawls or by our university affiliations. We reminisce about when Florida had a Christmas-to-Easter season and no Disney World. We may be split when it comes to our allegiance to the old days or adaptation to the new diversity flourishing in the state. Perhaps we feel we must choose sides. Fresh food or canned? Both can be nourishing. It is just a matter of taste.

For instance, when I was growing up, being a northerner was enough to be considered alien. Around my neighborhood, the talk was that black folks "up there" had to share apartments with strangers and sleep in shifts to pay their rent. And if you visited, you should not expect to be fed. Two of them might sit you down in the living room all "nicelike" to sip a drink. While one asked you about the family, the other one excused himself and ran back to the kitchen and ate just so they did not have to offer you some. That was an insult to a southerner. As a result of all I had heard, I did not make my first out-of-state trip, to New York, until I was well into my thirties. It was so traumatic that I suffered an attack of gall stones during the overnight train ride. My mind reeled from juggling all the warnings about how I should behave to hide my southern heritage: do not show your money; do not make eye contact; do not look up at tall buildings; do not ask directions. And whatever you do, do not say hello. That went counter to the tales of manners and propriety spun by neighborhood women when I was growing up. I realized how valuable one of the tales proved to be after I left the old community for college.

This story involved the black strangers who hovered on the periphery of our lives like shadows in the corners of our eyes. They collected dust and garbage from classrooms and roared polishing machines along the hallways of the dorm. An occasional brown hand behind the cafeteria table scooped up the special of the day and plopped it on our plates as we rushed along in line. But mostly they stayed out of our sight. To them we were trespassers, high-falutin' black outsiders who pushed ourselves into a place where we did not belong and were not wanted. They lived in a settlement of tract houses and farms around Gainesville when that bustling Central Florida community was still in an economic coma. The university was the town, their lifeblood employer, yet most of them had little chance of ever enrolling there. Still, I was the one who became starved for a glimpse of the familiar. When I caught sight of one of them as I strolled across campus, I dusted off my best Sunday-speaking manners and nodded hello with my lips skinned back into a smile. When the person nodded back to me or waved, I responded hungrily. As a child, on those porches and church steps, I learned that "speaking" was as much a cultural ritual as stories, a social courtesy that supersedes a handshake or exchange of business cards. Speaking invited conversation, but that was far better than appearing to intentionally snub someone. Even today, the black manager sometimes makes a point of nodding to the maintenance worker as they pass each other every day in the building, just to show he has not forgotten what he was taught. A black person walking with one or more whites may trade signals of acknowledgment with a black passerby. *I remember where I came from,* one of them telegraphs. *More power to you,* the other beams back. A simple courtesy.

The ritual crosses oceans and languages, too, I have discovered. A German companion and I boarded a city bus in Hamburg on one vacation and ambled toward the back. I was vaguely aware of someone sitting there, but as my companion leisurely sprawled out on the seat in front of me and we were deep in conversation, we could have been alone. Then a burst of energy hit me from behind. I thought I heard a low rumble, but it was almost indistinguishable. Still, it caught my attention enough to make me turn around. Right there, staring back, was a somber, darker face. "Hello, sister." The English was accented—not German, but African; the tone quiet, not prodding or even openly curious. I spoke, of course, and asked where he was from. Ghana. I said I was American. Acknowledgment. That was the most important thing. Then the exchange was over.

On a street outside my hotel in Paris, where I had stayed long enough to become comfortable with my surroundings, I headed out for the Metro one noon hour, wearing bright gold colors and with the spring-in-my-step feeling we women have when it is a good hair day. Smiling and nodding hellos as I made my way to the corner, I passed a short man with a dour expression headed the other way. I thought nothing of him—until I felt his energy slow down, stop, and spin around as he rushed back, retracing his steps to catch up with me. I had stopped at the intersection by then and was trapped, but the sidewalk was busy, so I felt reasonably safe until I could bolt to the other side. He talked up at me, fast and furious, in French, his expression never changing except for the urgency. My meager translation skills could not decipher all of his words, so I had to do a quick spot check for other signs. No passersby seemed to notice with alarm; no physical contact was made. In a matter of seconds, something in the steady stream of his words relaxed me into a smile again, once the scent of danger subsided. I began to realize what had caused him to break his stride. His look retained its seriousness, but he peppered his monologue with enough words for me to grasp the message. He had merely stopped to comment on my cordiality. "*Merci,*" he was saying, and I understood, as he abruptly bowed and walked away.

Lately when I am alone in a mall or walking a supermarket aisle or stopped at a traffic light, I have started applying the speaking ritual to children, who sorely need to be reminded that there are adults who are safe and not afraid of them. The little ones, regardless of race, usually smile shyly or wave. The startled black teenagers I greet sometimes as "gentlemen" when entering an elevator, for instance, look suddenly so young and vulnerable, if just for a moment. They hitch up their baggy pants and mumble a low-eyed, chin-down, shy-grinned response. Then I pretend not to notice the elbowing and shoving as one in the group corrals the others from stampeding long enough to make sure I *do* notice how they let me exit first. Maybe, decades from now, when some of those kids, about whose futures we make ominous predictions, recall these times as *their* good old days, they may tell some stories about the crazy lady who grinned and waved and made a spectacle of herself in public one day—over them. I do this selfishly, to remind myself that there are always some things we *can* affect in some way, however small, if we just keep working at it.

Some mornings I brew coffee at the oak-grained kitchen counter, as the deer on the rug stands guard in a silent watch behind me and as the sunlight does an early morning dance on the lake outside my window. And I think that maybe someday I might decide to stop traveling so much. I could end up trading the urban life for the pastoral, like my friend Louise, but I doubt that I would ever be content to sit back and weave tapestries for others to enjoy.

HEGIRAS

*T*he vacation was a lark—two midlife single women seeing some of the country by car for the first time. Traveling thirty-three hundred miles in eleven days, we wandered through small towns and strange cities, awakening more than memories. Some of the scenes could have been shot on a movie sound stage. They had all the elements. Trees blushed crimson and gold ahead of us against the backdrop of a cloudless fall sky. White houses and platted farms sprawled like a miniature set in the valleys below. Our silver convertible circled the mountains of Virginia and Pennsylvania, and even though we made seventy miles an hour, we seemed to be inching along. Elaine and I were contemporaries who shared some of the same tastes in media-created fantasies. We imagined ourselves to be like the two guys in the vintage television series *Route 66,* or the two women in the movie *Thelma and Louise,* but we had a spiritual mission in mind. When the last downbeat of Aretha Franklin's "Respect" faded out on the car's tape deck, I popped in a folksy Joni Mitchell cassette about escaping life and taking to the road. The angles of my friend's face hardened and her brown ponytail floated behind. I tightened the knot on my African head wrap as we headed toward New York City.

On this part of the drive north, we retraced her middle-class Jewish roots in an area of Brooklyn that had been underdeveloped during her youth in the 1950s and 1960s. We cruised over bridges, past waterfronts, restaurants, and residences, and I just enjoyed the pleasant scenery as she was reminded of various milestones in her life—the site of her first date, a teenage birthday party, a weekend family night outing. In this process of meandering, we took some side streets and wrong turns and ended up in Queens, at Howard Beach. The memories grew more poignant. "We had some good times here," she sighed, slowing down to crane her neck from side to side, hunting for an Italian eatery that was a landmark for some of her youthful escapades. A chill curled around me, shutting out the gaiety of her moment. I remembered the news reports I had heard about the young black man who was killed on that same highway as he was chased by a mob of angry whites simply because he dared to stop in their neighborhood to get a slice of pizza. And this incident had happened in the 1990s. Hatred has a long shelf life; it never goes out of style. And memories of its impact never completely fade. It was a comfort to know that the top of the car was up and locked down tight. I must have shuddered. In our household, I grew up hearing that a shudder meant someone was walking over the ground that would one day be your grave. Another Geechee saying, I guess. My friend rolled up the windows against the cool October air. I recounted the news report, trying to open a conversation about what I was feeling, but my words could never quite reach the depths of the incident. She listened but we didn't connect. She went back to her fond memories while I was left to wrestle in private with my reaction.

Later, on the trip back to Florida, we stopped by to say hello to a woman I had met at a difficult time in my life; she had been supportive when I was going through my divorce. Our relationship had continued long distance, by phone and letter, in part because of our common southern roots. We had used each other as sounding boards to sort out our tangled female roles and to talk candidly about our personal experiences with changing racial attitudes. As Elaine and I pulled up to her house we could see above an upstairs window a small Confederate flag alongside the Stars and Stripes. But when I introduced her to my traveling companion, I was caught in an unsettling white version of tribal war. The comment from our hostess sliced through the upbeat mood of the room, directed at both of her visitors with wide, innocent-looking eyes. "I don't know how you can stand it down there with all those pushy Jews," the woman said unknowingly. "It's not all of them, of course. But the ones in the Miami area, you know how they can be." My travel partner's mouth fell open and blood surged to a pounding in my ears. "That's not true," I interrupted, short-circuiting the conversation. "I'm not going to listen to that." But the damage was done. Within the next half-hour my friend and I had hit the road again, and I apologized sincerely for even inadvertently placing her in that situation. But a gnawing feeling flared up, something I could not quite identify, and it settled in for the rest of the ride.

Venturing off the interstate for awhile, we took the road over to St. Augustine; it would not have been my choice. My companion was charmed by the artsy character of the historic community that had sprung up around the schlocky "Fountain of Youth" and "Ripley's Believe It or Not" attractions that I vaguely recalled. "Let's come back for a weekend visit; it will be fun," she prodded, while I tried to shake off the bad memories of the racial clashes of the 1960s. This was the first time I had traveled that beach road since those turbulent times. I was just not convinced that enough had changed, even after all these years. We circled back north for a few miles with the flow of tourists' cars to get a closeup look at Jacksonville Beach, a first for me. As we stopped and parked near the boardwalk, I was startled to see a black man getting ready to exit from a nearby car, but then I began to feel a little less uneasy. Elaine suggested a meal at the restaurant overlooking the ocean. I decided against it, choosing to stroll along the ocean for a few minutes instead. A white family passing the other way nodded and waved to me pleasantly. The water shimmered gray-blue in the late morning light, just like at home in Fort Lauderdale, but the color seemed deeper, richer, and somehow more pronounced. So strong, in fact, I had to keep blinking as I stared, trying to squeeze this new reality into my mind. Twenty miles or so behind me lay the west side of town and a handful of relatives who had stayed there, but it might as well have been a lifetime away.

I could actually feel the great distance I had traveled, but it seems to me that many whites measure racial progress in small increments. If they drop a derogatory racial term from their vocabulary or accept someone from another race as a house guest, a date, or even a brief lover, they boast that their lives have been transformed. *Stick a toe in the water and claim you are wet.* Blacks, on the other hand, often feel that they are expected to display a hypersensitivity to indignities committed against other people but that they risk being accused of anger or militancy if they express a deeply personal outrage. *Stay separate and you save yourself a lot of grief.* The complexities of these racial feelings rose up and loomed there once again in a gap that sometimes appeared without warning; I fought against the sudden undertow.

Moments of daylight, of clarity, can come just as swiftly sometimes, however. On a different journey sometime later, my first visit to New Orleans, I traveled with two other women friends. We planned to spend a Saturday touring some plantations outside the city. One of my friends guided the rental car carefully along winding roads licked lightly with rain. The other sat in the back seat loading her video camera. Armed with a tourist map from the hotel, I matched the flagged locations with the landmarks and signs. I admit I was doing only a half-hearted job. I had prepared myself to concentrate on the endurance of nature as I walked around grandfather oaks still spreading their ancient shade on what was once an antebellum lawn. I would fake interest in the architecture as I passed the white columns and wraparound porches and climbed the stairs to peek into rooms decorated with nineteenth-century antiques. I knew the tour guide would avoid my eyes as he pointed out the backyard garden maze and the kitchen beyond. From there the food and drink would be transferred, rain or shine, by the "servants," he would say, rushing past the last word before changing the subject. I would be on the lookout for some remnant of the "servants'" quarters, but in the grand homes where we stopped, any trace of the slaves once forced to work there had somehow disappeared. I thought I hid my restlessness well, waiting outside the gift shop until it was time to leave. My keen-eyed friends, both with roots firmly planted—one in her family's Italian heritage and the other in four generations of southern, Florida soil—insisted on photographs of me looking out over the grounds of one of the plantation homes and standing at the front door, waving a welcome like plantation mistress.

Periodically, over one of our birthday lunches at home, we shared stories about families. When one of my friends made the mistake of asking what part of Africa my ancestors were from, I testily reminded the interrogator that I did not know. Despite the colorful touches of African customs and folklore in my upbringing, the Geechee represented an amalgam, a new creation from a mixture of old ways. Unable to learn more about that part of my family tree, I had to settle for visiting Thomas Jefferson's home, Boston's African Meeting Hall and Museum, and monuments to the Underground Railway like so many other African Americans searching secondhand for a sense of identity, a sense of place. The marooned, looking for glimpses of home.

As these friends and I headed back to our New Orleans hotel in the late afternoon, I felt a tug on the heart, as strong as a wake-up call that rouses one from a dream. I wanted to see where my ancestors had lived, I told my friends. Poring over the map, we finally found a sign and a turn that led to a clearing, where we found three modest buildings that looked more like a cottage and two cabins. The mother-daughter team of operators explained that this plantation property was in transition. A replica of the main house, which had burned down many years ago, was being built. A guest house, a carriage house, and a workhouse remained. The workhouse, where slaves one slept, was actually two one-room shacks that in modern times had been shoved together to create the look of a modestly furnished dining room and bedroom. Sheer curtains prettied up a back window. None of this was true to the period, admitted the daughter part of the team. During the days of slavery, each of the walk-in, closet-sized rooms had only pallets on the floor. Men and women slept there, twenty or thirty a night, sandwiched in, expected to breed more slaves for their owners. She explained all this reluctantly, after some prodding for details. Of course, I knew this, but still it was difficult to stand in such a spot and hear that truth. Even in January, with just four of us, heat wrapped itself so strong and tight around the room that my friend with the video camera had to leave. I stood rooted there, my pulse rising as I imagined what it must have been like for those men and women to writhe in that close, dark pit without even a view of the moon watching with its nightly eyes. What sad, hopeful rhythms their bodies must have created, birthing out of desolation generations of black children they would never live to see, what progress they would never live to make. The videotape of that afternoon records only the silence of tears that fell freely from my friends' eyes and mine. But what I remember most is, buried beneath a hug, the muffled voice of one of them in my ear, whispering softly, "I'm so sorry," as we walked back to the car.

We still talk about that experience sometimes, and the bond it created, during our lunches on back-porch afternoons, hiding from the South Florida sun. With the ease of family we still talk about race, too, in a healing way. In those moments, I stretch out on the couch, relaxed and unguarded, my face kissed by the wind. I am still aware, all the same, that on this multicolored journey, I am a guest without a true home. Even in private, subconsciously I live that way. My bed is made every morning as soon as I arise. The newspapers are read, then refolded neatly and stored away. Once the afternoon mail has been sorted in the living room, the coffee table is promptly cleared of all clutter. In the evenings when I have nothing else to do, I play the hard-to-please decorator. Wicker chairs and end tables are separated, regrouped, and reintroduced. Striped and flowered throw pillows are mixed and matched. Candles here, a silk plant there, a centerpiece, some groupings of books are all straightened and angled several times as I try for just the right effect. After one last critical check, I add the finishing touches, then sit in various spots around the room admiring the compact, lightly furnished design. As I sip coffee with satisfaction, a thought zips through my mind, fast and palpable as an ocean breeze. *What a lovely place I have created for someone.* Then I shake my head to clear it, because this is *mine,* and *I* live here.

In the outside world, my professional life is a daily crazy quilt of to-do lists on different-sized yellow Post-it notes, thoughts scribbled on the back of old letterhead, and words and ideas doodled into blocks and triangles that turn into clown faces. I juggle so many projects at one time that my friends say it gives them a headache just to think about it. By contrast, these at-home rituals are curious, even to me. My house is undeniably filled with mementoes I treasure. It is the refuge to which I cannot wait to escape when life gets too stressful and complicated. Sure, I have been saddled with the baggage that ownership can bring, problems I have inherited from other people and either learned to tolerate or managed to fix. But a piece of me has been forever embedded in these walls. Still, I am reluctant to say I am settled, that this is "home." As far back as I can remember, I have always felt that word belonged in other people's vocabulary or applied to some place other than where I was.

At the door of Oak Alley plantation outside New Orleans, 1999.

As a five-year-old, I watched my mother dress before the mirror to go out at night after a hardworking day until I grew drowsy under the blanket of her sweet perfume. But when the locks on the door clicked behind her, my imagination sped ahead. The sound I heard was night crawling

Overlooking the grounds of restored Oak Alley plantation.

through a crack in the window, pushing aside the curtains and breathing so intensely that I had to pull the bedspread over my head to make it go away. One night I discovered that if I turned on the light, fear took on a shape and form. The rustling I heard turned out to be cockroach wings that roared past my head like secrets startled out of their hiding place. When I grabbed one of my brown oxfords and chased after them, they scattered guiltily. I even killed a few. I never told Mama the story about the cockroaches, but she must have gotten a hint. She began leaving the light on, and we did not stay in that apartment long. I slept more easily, as we moved often during those early years, by creating safe, pretty, movie-star places in my dreams.

Janice, my best friend throughout high school, lived in a split-level house, not an A-frame, with a washer and dryer instead of a clothesline. Her skirts and blouses hung in wall-to-wall closets instead of on wire hangers suspended from nails on the backs of doors. Her daddy was the first black man hired to work for the city; her mother, a housewife. In the afternoons, we danced to the jazz piano of Ahmad Jamal's "Poinciana" and talked on Princess extension phones. I vowed that one day I would recreate what I saw in a house just like that—a cocoon of love. They only allowed me to see a few of their rooms, and when it was time for family dinner, I always had to leave.

Displacement was ingrained in me early, I guess, and it has been an uneasy travel companion through the years. Perhaps the roots are cultural. For instance, even today when a black person, especially from the South, asks me, "Where are you from?" I know the point is not to reminisce about the good old days in the old neighborhood. The conversation might start there, as the town, the street corners, and the major landmarks are named and the questioner tries to make a connection by inquiring about the schools or churches in the vicinity. But the talk shifts quickly to what matters: do we know any of the same people? Maybe we will strike gold and find that we are distantly related. There is the tacit acknowledgment that, of course, we have come "from" somewhere else, historically speaking, and that place no longer exists. All our other stops along the way have been pretty much transitory. That fact makes it more difficult—for me, anyway—to share in the wistful sense of attachment to one place that so many people feel.

I married someone "from" my hometown, and we spent our first several years living in South Florida while plotting to move to California. We had an illusion that California was the place where life was liberal, open-minded, and free. We could mingle with musicians, writers, and celebrities and find work easily. There, we could rent an apartment without having to threaten a discrimination lawsuit. We could buy a house in a neighborhood where whites would not sell out and flee. Race would not matter as much as it did in the South. But hatred knows no geographical boundaries. I started encountering transplants to Florida from California, joining the northerners, midwesterners, and people from just about every other corner of the globe. So relatively speaking, I have stayed put. Nevertheless, within the confines of one county, I have moved many times: from a large city of boulevards, avenues, terraces, courts, and lanes; to a smaller scenic town of streets with presidents' names; to a western community of horse trails and bird watchers, minutes from the Everglades. Here, in a condo, I sit longing for a house along the eastern shore with the smell of saltwater and sand. When I think about "home" as the place of my origins, the idea takes on a surreal quality. Memory tends to paint the past with bright colors. Moments stand out with significance and sometimes seem even more vivid than the bland canvas of day-to-day life. Good times become golden; rough times, the darkest blues.

On one of my return visits to Jacksonville not too long ago, I took a drive through some of the old familiar areas on my own, straying from the main roads I usually take when driving Mama around on errands. I wanted to get a visual recap of the place that had become such a staple of my writing at this stage of my life. I traveled along uneven brick roads, past a few landmark houses with peeling paint and loose screens, leaning like old men with time. Much of what I remember has been torn down to make way for expressways and wider streets or has been demolished, leaving a gaping hole. The original marquee of just one old movie theater has survived after decades of neglect, rising in red neon like a fake phoenix, but it is just an outer shell for the modern meeting hall inside. The old high school looks the same, or as much as I can remember of it from those years when I was longing to leave. It has an award-winning magnet program that has helped it survive changing times. When the bell rang during one of my more recent visits, students flowed into the hallway, more white faces than black ones. No one knew the few old teachers I recalled. In a storage room full of boxes, alumni older and younger than I stare out of yearbooks from the early and late 1960s, the 1970s, and beyond. The library does not even have a yearbook from my class of 1965, when a generation began its pivot toward integration, but at least we have our memories.

Memory can afford to be kind because it is limited in what it sees. Most things look better in a distant light. When I go back to some of my old South Florida neighborhoods, where I first learned to drive our brand-new 1970 Maverick or where my children played ball in the streets long past dark, I can still find my way in and out of traffic congestion with a sharp turn down a road I recognize. I remember once weaving easily around curves without stop signs and barriers and passing houses that were well kept and well lit. Now I hit cul-de-sacs that wreathe around and cut off like ribbons with knots, and the streets are hardly safe. Familiarity with a place is not enough to make it feel permanent.

I am in a place now where a blanket of quiet settles on the street outside as I head for bed. The room is a dusky floral nest of books, scenic pastels, and potpourri. The small pillows are tucked away beside the dresser, the larger ones stacked by the door, the shams fluffed and ready for morning, when duty calls them all again. Drifting off, I catch a whiff of something spicy from the top of a chest of drawers, out of sight, where a holder sits with a rose-colored candle. I bought it not too long ago from a little country store in my neighborhood where I occasionally shop, but I had forgotten about it. And I laugh despite myself as I remember that the owner told me it was a new product. *It's called "Home,"* she said. I fall asleep to the subtle scent.